THE
PRUSSIAN
PRINCESSES

THE SISTERS OF
KAISER WILHELM II

THE PRUSSIAN PRINCESSES

THE SISTERS OF KAISER WILHELM II

JOHN VAN DER KISTE

FONTHILL

Fonthill Media Language Policy

Fonthill Media publishes in the international English language market. One language edition is published worldwide. As there are minor differences in spelling and presentation, especially with regard to American English and British English, a policy is necessary to define which form of English to use. The Fonthill Policy is to use the form of English native to the author. John Van der Kiste was born and educated in England, therefore British English has been adopted in this publication.

Fonthill Media Limited
Fonthill Media LLC
www.fonthillmedia.com
office@fonthillmedia.com

First published in the United Kingdom
and the United States of America 2014

British Library Cataloguing in Publication Data:
A catalogue record for this book is available from the British Library

Copyright © John Van der Kiste 2014

ISBN 978-1-78155-443-2

Typeset in 10.5pt on 13pt Sabon
Printed and bound by CPI Group (UK) Ltd, Croydon, CR0 4YY

Contents

Genealogical Table

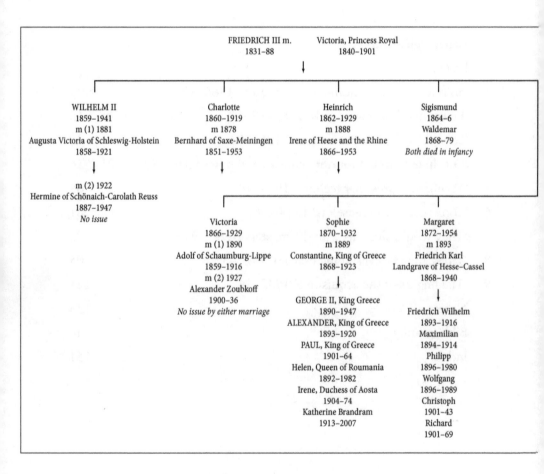

FRIEDRICH III m.   Victoria, Princess Royal
1831–88   1840–1901

WILHELM II	Charlotte	Heinrich	Sigismund
1859–1941	1860–1919	1862–1929	1864–6
m (1) 1881	m 1878	m 1888	Waldemar
Augusta Victoria of Schleswig-Holstein	Bernhard of Saxe-Meiningen	Irene of Heese and the Rhine	1868–79
1858–1921	1851–1953	1866–1953	*Both died in infancy*

m (2) 1922
Hermine of Schönaich-Carolath Reuss
1887–1947
No issue

Victoria	Sophie	Margaret
1866–1929	1870–1932	1872–1954
m (1) 1890	m 1889	m 1893
Adolf of Schaumburg-Lippe	Constantine, King of Greece	Friedrich Karl
1859–1916	1868–1923	Landgrave of Hesse–Cassel
m (2) 1927		1868–1940
Alexander Zoubkoff		
1900–36	GEORGE II, King Greece	Friedrich Wilhelm
No issue by either marriage	1890–1947	1893–1916
	ALEXANDER, King of Greece	Maximilian
	1893–1920	1894–1914
	PAUL, King of Greece	Philipp
	1901–64	1896–1980
	Helen, Queen of Roumania	Wolfgang
	1892–1982	1896–1989
	Irene, Duchess of Aosta	Christoph
	1904–74	1901–43
	Katherine Brandram	Richard
	1913–2007	1901–69

Preface

Having started my career as a royal biographer with Kaiser Friedrich III, and later written about Emperor Wilhelm II as well as producing a joint study of his parents, it was inevitable that in due course I would turn the spotlight on the princesses. I wrote a short account of the relationship between the eldest daughter Charlotte, Hereditary Princess of Saxe-Meiningen, and her only child Feodora, Princess Heinrich of Reuss, and then started one on Friedrich's second daughter, Victoria, who became Princess Adolf of Schaumburg-Lippe, and later briefly but disastrously Madame Zoubkoff. It soon became apparent that a joint biography of her and her younger siblings, Sophie, Queen of Greece, and Margaret, Landgravine of Hesse-Cassel—their mother's Kleeblatt or trio as she affectionately called them—would result in a much more interesting work for readers, as well as a far more enjoyably challenging one to write.

In a book of this nature, the royal biographer is inevitably faced with the question of whether to refer to his or her subjects throughout by their family nicknames or not. Moretta, Sossy, and Mossy are unique and therefore less confusing, but arguably too trite and, some would say, bordering on the disrespectful. Then there is the issue with German royalty of the English or German form. After some deliberation I have tried to take a middle course and use the German names, while respecting the convention of retaining the Anglicised 'Empress Frederick' as preferable for British readers to 'Kaiserin Friedrich'. The Landgrave of Hesse-Cassel signed her letters to her friend Lady Corkran with the name Margaret, and I have preferred this to the German 'Margrethe'. I have made Victoria 'young Vicky' during the earlier years, in order to minimise confusion between her and the other Victorias, her mother, and her grandmother. Moreover, at the risk of inaccuracy, Wilhelm II is referred to as Emperor throughout the narrative, even after his abdication.

I am grateful to the following for their encouragement, assistance, and provision of illustrations and other material: Mark Andersen; Marlene Eilers; Julia P. Gelardi; Coryne Hall; Kori Roff Lawrence; Eric Lowe; Ilana D. Miller; Karen Roth; Ian Shapiro of Argyll Etkin Ltd; Katrina Warne; Sue Woolmans; Charlotte Zeepvat; and various regular contributors to the Royal Books Facebook page. Hilary Clare performed a sterling task in her research on my behalf of Princess Margaret's letters to Lady Corkran in the Bodleian Library, and I am happy to acknowledge her hard work and record my thanks for her permission to make use of the material. Last but by no means least, thanks are due to my wife Kim for her ever-present assistance and reading of the manuscript in draft form, and to my editor, Constance Long, for her help at the final pre-publication stages.

1

'So full of understanding of us children' 1866–83

On 25 January 1858, Victoria, Princess Royal, the eldest daughter of Queen Victoria and Prince Albert, married Prince Friedrich Wilhelm of Prussia, son of Prince Wilhelm and Princess Augusta, at St James's Chapel, London. The bride was only aged seventeen, while the groom was nine years older than her at twenty-six. As second in succession to the throne of Prussia after his father Wilhelm, heir to the childless King Friedrich Wilhelm IV—both of whom were in their sixties—he was confidently expected to become King himself before very long.

Their first child, Wilhelm, was born one year later, on 27 January 1859. At the end of a traumatic pregnancy, there was a long and difficult confinement in which mother and child almost died; the baby—apparently left for dead during the first few minutes of his life—was born with a deformed left hand and arm, as well as possible brain damage. Yet the princess was an extremely maternal young woman who had set her heart on having a large family, and this first unpleasant experience of childbirth did not put her off having seven more children. The first of four daughters, Charlotte, was born on 24 July 1860, followed by two more sons, Heinrich on 14 August 1862, and Sigismund on 15 September 1864.

By the autumn of 1865, Crown Princess Friedrich Wilhelm of Prussia, as she had then become with the death of the King and accession to the throne of her father-in-law Wilhelm in January 1861, was expecting her fifth child the following spring. On 12 April 1866, she travelled by train from Berlin to the Neue Palais, Potsdam, their summer home, where confinement was due to take place. Her labour began during the journey, and at one point her attendants feared that she might even give birth on the train. Fortunately, they reached Potsdam just in time, only to find that nothing was ready, and the nurse who had been chosen to supervise matters during the confinement was still on her way from Berlin. There were no baby clothes at hand for the child, and the only item to be found in the palace to wrap her in was an old petticoat.[1]

The birth of the new princess occurred at a difficult time for her parents and her country. Prussia was preparing for war with Austria over a dispute concerning the administration of the duchies of Schleswig and Holstein; the Crown Princess's worry over the situation may have accounted for her premature labour. Crown Prince Friedrich Wilhelm had been appointed to take up command with the Second Army in Silesia, and was due to leave on the day after his daughter's christening. This had been arranged to take place on 24 May, the birthday of the baby's grandmother, Queen Victoria, after whom she was to be named. The Crown Princess wrote gloomily to her mother a few days earlier:

> Our christening will be such a sad one, the day after my Fritz leaves and joins his troops ... when and where I shall see him again I do not know, what I feel I cannot tell you. I think my heart will break. All is uncertain, and ruin and misfortune of every kind likely.[2]

The baby was christened Frederica Amalia Wilhelmina Victoria. A few weeks later, the Crown Princess faced her first loss of a child when her youngest son, Sigismund, aged twenty-one months, succumbed to meningitis. He died in agony on 16 June, without proper medical care as most doctors had been called to the battlefront to tend to wounded soldiers. 'I am calm now,' she wrote to her mother three days later '– for Fritz's sake and my little ones—but oh! how bitter is the cross'.[3] Sigismund was the first of Queen Victoria's forty-two grandchildren to die.

The first few weeks of the baby princess's life were naturally overshadowed by the loss of the elder brother whom she had never known. In July, her mother sent the Queen a photograph of the child of three months, known in the family as 'little Vicky'. She added in her letter that the baby was

> such a dear, pretty, little thing, and so lively; she crows, laughs and jumps and begins to sit up and has short petticoats. If I was not continually reminded of what we had lost I should enjoy her so much and be proud of her too.[4]

An intense bereavement over Sigismund's death continued to haunt the Crown Princess. A year later she sent another, somewhat macabre photograph to the Queen, calling it a bad picture of her youngest daughter: 'she has on the little garden hat and jacket her little brother wore so much last year; they are the things he had on when he was taken ill.'[5] By this time the Queen was becoming alarmed by her daughter's strange behaviour, which nowadays might have been diagnosed as some kind of nervous breakdown. She wrote firmly to tell her that she found it distressing to see pictures of the child dressed in those clothes, saying that she would 'have a superstitious feeling about putting another living child into the clothes which had been worn by one who was dead. I say all this in love and affection.'[6]

Her words evidently had the right effect. After this there would be little more if anything heard on such a morbid subject, and at last the Crown Princess could try and put the bereavement behind her. As a baby, little Victoria was placed under the care of a British nurse, Mrs Hobbs, who taught her to speak English. At the age of two she could not or would not speak a word of the language of her own country. As the Crown Princess noted, she was 'the only one of our children who does not speak German, she will not say any German words'.[7]

Little Victoria was also very shy, and her mother reported that when she was aged only two she would not even look at a stranger; instead, she would hide her face in her mother's gown or that of Mrs Hobbs and roar 'at the top of her voice'.[8] This might have been due to a disturbing incident in May 1868, when a lunatic broke into the nurseries at the Neue Palais. A footman managed to overpower him before he could reach the children's bedrooms, but little Vicky was awoken by the noise and screamed in terror.

It was not the only unpleasant domestic misadventure of her earliest years. Almost two years later, in February 1870, a fire broke out in the middle of the night at the Berlin palace, filling the corridors and landings with flames and black smoke. The family and their servants were quickly evacuated, but all suffered from shock. A couple of months after that, another madman jumped into a carriage in which the princess, her brother, and sisters were being taken for a drive. He tried to settle himself down in the lap of Mrs Hawes, the nurse, and refused to leave the carriage. The children were helped out but the man bit the footman's hand when he attempted to remove him; a struggle ensued and he was eventually marched away.[9] It turned out that he was a native of Bohemia with mental health issues, and he had previously done much the same thing on the streets of Vienna, when he harassed the little Archduchess Gisela, daughter of Emperor Franz Josef of Austria.

In February 1868 the Crown Princess had a fourth son, Waldemar. Two years later her third daughter, like her second, would arrive amid the shadows of impending war. The family were at the Neue Palais for the confinement on 14 June 1870, at the height of tension between Prussia and France over the possibility of a Hohenzollern candidate being offered the throne of Spain. The unpopular Queen Isabella had abdicated, and at one stage it looked as if she would be replaced by Prince Leopold of Hohenzollern-Sigmaringen, a distant cousin of King Wilhelm of Prussia, from the Catholic branch of the family. Leopold decided not to accept the crown, but Otto von Bismarck, Minister-President of Prussia, had been waiting for a pretext to declare war against France and unite the North German Confederation in victory, and thereby create a new German Empire with Prussia at the helm.

Hostilities were declared in July, the same month that the third little princess was christened Sophie Dorothea Ulrica Alice amid traditional pomp and ceremony. Most of the men present wore their military uniforms; among them were Sophie's father and Bismarck, attired as a Major of the Prussian Dragoons. It was a sad ceremony, the Crown Princess reported to her mother: 'anxious faces and tearful eyes, and a gloom and foreshadowing of all the misery in store spread a serious cloud over the ceremony, which should have been one of gladness and thanksgiving.'[10] Early next morning, before the rest of the family were awake, the Crown Prince left quietly to join his troops. One German victory followed another, and in January 1871 the German Empire was declared at the Hall of Mirrors, Versailles. King Wilhelm of Prussia was now German Kaiser, a new exalted honour which he had never really wanted.

That summer, the German Crown Princess was expecting another child, and she was deeply hurt when her mother-in-law Empress Augusta chose to break the news to Queen Victoria herself. Although the Crown Princess had already had seven children, this time she admitted to her mother that for once she was 'horribly afraid of the event'. She felt 'very nervous about it, as there is nothing I can do in the way of walking or diet or anything to make me have an easier time, and those very hard ones such as with Waldemar & Sophie are really dreadful.'[11] Queen Victoria's sympathy with her daughter proved somewhat limited, as she replied to say how sorry she was that she was unwell in the latter stages of pregnancy, but that it was no surprise. 'I only hope & pray you will be satisfied when you have 7,' she wrote sternly, '& not go on exhausting your health & strength which is so precious to all you belong to & so necessary to your husband & children & to your adopted country.'[12]

The child, a fourth daughter, was born on 22 April 1872. The Crown Princess was initially disappointed, as she told Queen Victoria:

> If it had been a boy I should have hoped with you for it to have been the youngest for evermore, as really what one has to endure is too wretched, but it would be wrong of me to complain, and for myself alone a little girl is much nicer, and she will be a companion for Sophie.[13]

This baby had 'an immense lot of dark hair'.[14] She was christened Margaret Beatrice Feodora: the first name in honour of Margherita, Crown Princess of Italy, who like her husband Crown Prince Umberto had been asked to be among the godparents; Beatrice after her aunt; and Feodora in memory of Queen Victoria's half-sister, who had died two months earlier. By the time of the christening, her head was covered in short hair, which her mother thought looked rather like a clump of moss, and she was therefore nicknamed Mossy.

Queen Victoria strongly urged that this one should remain the baby for some time. The Crown Princess felt that she owed Germany another son, but she was disinclined to go through a ninth confinement, as her mother had done, and the fourth girl was indeed destined to be the youngest of the family.

The children were brought up between the two homes of their parents, the palace at Unter den Linden, Berlin, and the Neue Palais at Potsdam. Crown Princess Victoria was allowed more of a free hand in the upbringing of her younger children than she had with the elder siblings, and she recognised that young Vicky and those who had followed her would always be much closer to their parents. A few years earlier they had purchased a more informal property in the village of Bornstadt, near Potsdam. For the small girl, and her brothers and sisters, here was a place with a model farm, country air, and simple pleasures, far removed from the formality of life in Berlin. To a certain extent this was their equivalent of Osborne House, the home that Queen Victoria and Prince Albert had purchased on the Isle of Wight.

The Crown Princess was a very affectionate mother, passionately fond of small children in a way that Queen Victoria had never been. On Mossy's first birthday she wrote of the baby to Queen Victoria as 'such a little love—so forward, so pretty, and so good, I think she would find favour in your eyes in spite of being my pet.'[15] Seven years later, she noted that her youngest daughter was

such a love, such a little sunbeam, so good and so gifted, she will be a charming little person one day, but sometimes I fear not a very happy one, for she is so sensitive and her little heart so tender and warm and loving, so clinging that she is sure to suffer a good deal through life—as those must whose feelings are deep and keen, and who have much love to bestow.[16]

At the same time, the Crown Princess could be quite demanding in her expectations. She watched over the behaviour, development, and education of all her children with keen interest and constant vigilance—something which brought her into conflict with the traditions and conventions of the Prussian court. She always maintained that she would be failing in her duty if she 'abandoned' her natural right as a mother to have some say in the education of her children, and she had every right to judge for herself what they were to learn and who was to teach them. This brought her into conflict with her unbending parents-in-law, King Wilhelm and Queen Augusta, who had become German Kaiser and Empress in January 1871. In their view, such an attitude would surely encroach on their rights to involve themselves in the upbringing of their grandchildren.

Sophie and Mossy did not leave any memoirs, and it is to a volume written by 'little Vicky', published towards the end of her life in 1929, that posterity is indebted for little glimpses into their childhood and upbringing, even though they were almost inevitably viewed through rose-tinted spectacles. Even so, she was prepared to admit that she had mixed feelings about her paternal grandparents. While she recalled that King Wilhelm had always been 'kind and simple', her earliest recollection of the sharp-tempered Queen Augusta were the words, 'You do not scamper!' when she was running out of a room at three years old.[17]

The King and Queen had never enjoyed a happy marriage or a particularly close bond with their son and daughter-in-law. They took some interest in their three elder grandchildren, but on the whole they ignored the younger ones, whom they considered to be less important. In contrast, the children received a much warmer welcome from their grandmother in England, Queen Victoria, and their mother regularly took them to stay there. Their favourite home was Osborne House, and the youngsters immersed themselves in the island's charms, where they loved to walk along the beaches and collect shells. Victoria spoke for her younger sisters as well as herself when she mentioned that their English grandmother was 'always so gracious and kind, and so full of understanding of us children'.[18] Sophie was especially taken with the Queen, and her mother allowed her to stay for long periods in England. After a visit in the summer of 1881, the Crown Princess wrote to her mother that 'the children are so full of dear Grandmama and all her kindness that it does my heart good, "and," says Sophie, "she is so nice to kiss you cannot think".'[19]

Their grandfather's birthday was always celebrated the same way. On 22 March each year, the whole family took their place in state coaches to ride to the palace in Berlin where they would offer him their congratulations. The young princesses curtseyed and kissed his hand, after which he would gently withdraw it and fondly stroke their faces. Seven months later, on 18 October, the Crown Prince's birthday, they would hold a grand ball in the evening for their friends and court officials.

When the children were old enough, probably at the age of four or five, they began to take lessons at home. These started at eight o'clock in the morning and were followed by breakfast with their parents an hour later. The rest of the day, with breaks for further meals, was occupied mostly with further lessons and periods of exercise, according to the time of year. The latter activities included skating, swimming, rowing, riding, gymnastics, dancing, and tennis, and this last game became a lifelong passion with little Vicky. She was never academically inclined, and would readily admit that she had always been a difficult and reluctant pupil; her interests were much more in outdoor life and sports of every kind than in learning and study.[20]

The children's teachers were all chosen with great care. Little Vicky's favourite governess was Miss Byng, who she called 'Minnie' and considered a second mother. She also got on well with her German governess, Fraülein Poppe, who, being very musical and fond of singing, gave her young charge her first singing lessons and taught her German nursery songs. Her brother Heinrich would come along to the schoolroom and join in in what she considered were some of the most enjoyable lessons they ever had.

Three governesses were resident in the palace, led by Mademoiselle de Perpignan. She delegated duties to the others and was in effect their headmistress. One of her tasks was to help the princesses take care of their pocket money, which she kept in a leather bag always tied round her waist, even when she was wearing evening dress. Vicky was fascinated by the fact that she had hair of extraordinary length—down to her knees—and when she asked how Mademoiselle did it, she replied that she washed it in brandy, which struck the young girl as very extravagant. Their French lessons were supervised by Mademoiselle Bujard, and Vicky was not a conscientious pupil. She admitted to being lazy and sulked when the poor woman lost her temper. One day, the governess declared she had had enough, put on her hat and coat, and said that she was going away for good. Having made her point, she returned quietly to find little Vicky disconsolate in her room. Abject apologies and forgiveness followed, and they became friends again.[21]

Like her mother had done at a much earlier age, the Princess quickly learned how to answer back. Whenever a music governess scolded her for misbehaving, she would retort, 'The Bible says, "Love your enemies!"' A history tutor, calling her for her lesson, was informed rather haughtily that her arrangements for the day were not yet complete. At this he struck the table so fiercely with a ruler that it broke, and a pot of red ink was upset over the carpet. She fled from the room into the arms of a governess, who thought she was having hysterics, and fetched her a glass of magnesia.[22]

Princess Victoria's favourite childhood activities were dancing, for which she took lessons every Saturday, and riding. One of her first mounts was Alfred, a little Shetland pony that had been a gift to her from Queen

Victoria, much to the envy of her brothers. Although she was only aged five when he arrived at the stables in Germany, she took to him at once, and enjoyed getting on his back and galloping around the grounds of the Neue Palais. One day she was riding him when Wilhelm and Heinrich were sitting outside nearby, thoroughly bored by their drawing lesson and more than ready for a little distraction. As they caught sight of their younger sister, they began throwing small pebbles at Alfred. One of them hit him and he kicked violently. She was thrown out of the saddle and landed on her head on the ground. Wilhelm ran up to her, thoroughly alarmed, and found her unhurt but very angry. He penitently placed her back in the saddle.[23]

Throughout childhood, little Vicky was always affectionate and generally well-behaved. In March 1878 she was confirmed. In a letter to Queen Victoria, the Crown Princess described the proceedings, attended by the younger children, with Sophie and Mossy in blue satin slips with the Isle of Wight lace their grandmother had given them, each holding a nosegay. She remarked to her mother that Vicky, now aged eleven, had tact and discretion far beyond her years:

> [I am] often astonished at the true, tender-hearted little woman she is in feeling. She has such a sweet disposition. I shall never feel anxious on her account, if she is but spared! One could trust her anywhere.[24]

Little Vicky, Sophie and Mossy, and their brother Waldemar, were all devoted to their parents. The four of them formed a close family unit, noticeably at odds with that of the three eldest children, who had been far more influenced by the Prussian court, brought up partly by others, and taught to view the 'English' ways of both their parents with contempt.

Waldemar was an affectionate boy with winning ways. He and Little Vicky used to have their arithmetic lessons together, which they found very dull. Once the lesson was over, they would race noisily down the palace corridor, playfully throwing the books at each other's heads.[25] He was the kind of child who could be naughty but get away with anything through sheer charm. He was devoted to animals, and this love of pets did not stop at cats and dogs. On one visit to England to stay with Queen Victoria, he took Bob, his pet crocodile. One evening, monarch and pachyderm unexpectedly came face to face, and she screamed in terror until Waldemar came to pick him up and take him out of the room, almost helpless with laughter at the effect it had had on her.

Waldemar's death from diphtheria in March 1879, a month after his eleventh birthday, was a blow to the family from which his mother never really recovered. After that the division between the three elder and the three younger children gradually widened. The Crown Princess had been allowed more control over the upbringing of her younger children, and after the tragic deaths of her two younger sons, she clung more to the daughters. Young Vicky, Sophie, and Mossy drew closer still to their parents. To the Crown Princess, they were 'my three sweet girls', her trio, or *Kleeblatt*. Their eldest brother Wilhelm disparagingly dubbed them 'the English colony', and he claimed that under their mother's upbringing they did not seem like Germans, but had become excessively anglophilic.

The summer after Waldemar's death, the girls and their mother were bitterly upset when a tabby cat he had acquired as a kitten, and of which they were all particularly fond, was killed by a gamekeeper. Seeing the little animal in the garden, he deliberately shot her, hung her up on a tree and cut off her nose. They got no sympathy from Wilhelm, who had no sentimental feelings towards pets and the matter of owning them, and defended the keeper on the grounds that cats often harmed pheasants.[26] The sisters tried to comfort themselves as best they could by burying the cat in their late brother's garden, alongside the grave of a dachshund which had been accidentally driven over.

Ever keen to be useful, and encouraged by suggestions from her mother, young Vicky decided she would like to learn the basics of cookery. At the first lesson, one of her contemporaries, Marie von Bunsen, a lady-in-waiting, saw that the princess's enthusiasm was not matched by her knowledge. Marie asked her to watch a pan of water on the stove and let her know when it came to the boil. Little Vicky promised she would do so, but there was one problem: how, she asked, would she know when it was boiling? This was one anecdote that she omitted from her memoirs.

It was only to be expected that Vicky was prouder of her ability to prepare spinach. Once, she brought some vegetables home to her parents to taste, and was very gratified when they praised them. 'Uncle Fritz Karl', the Kaiser's younger brother Friedrich Karl, was equally appreciative of her skills. He told his great-niece that he had never eaten better-cooked spinach in his life.[27]

2

'I have my three sweet girls'
1883–89

By the time she reached adolescence, Victoria had become a striking if not particularly attractive young woman. She was the tallest of the sisters, with a naturally dark complexion and a tendency to tan easily in the sun. At around this time her name in the family changed from Vicky or 'young Vicky' to Moretta. Exactly how this name came about is uncertain, but it has been suggested that it was derived from an Italian word, either a term of endearment or a region of Piedmont, and at the same time it could refer to a young woman who was dark-haired or dark-skinned. It would have been natural for the Crown Prince and Princess to choose an Italian-inspired pet name, as they were both fond of the country and its royal family. At the same time, Moretta was considered an incurable Romantic, possibly even something of a flirt by some. Her elder sister, the frivolous, party-loving Charlotte, had been married in February 1878, at the age of seventeen, to Prince Bernhard of Saxe-Meiningen, and the question of a suitable husband for Moretta now had to be considered as well.

Among the most eligible bachelor princes of the age throughout Europe were the good-looking sons of Prince Alexander of Hesse. They had only one serious disadvantage in the eyes of some, in that they were of insufficiently royal birth. In 1851 their father had made a morganatic marriage with Countess Julie von Hauke, a former lady-in-waiting to the late Empress Marie of Russia, and as a result they had been banished from the Russian court. Their eldest son Louis, born the following year, had joined the British navy, and in June 1883 he became betrothed to one of Queen Victoria's eldest granddaughters, Victoria of Hesse and the Rhine. In addition to Louis there were three younger brothers: Alexander ('Sandro'), sovereign Prince of Bulgaria; Heinrich, who would later become the Queen's son-in-law; and Franz Josef. They were all noted for their good looks. The Queen, it appears, was probably the first to suggest that Alexander might make a suitable husband for her granddaughter Moretta.

For his part, Alexander was keen to find a suitably connected bride who, through their marriage and children, would strengthen his position as ruler of the rather unstable principality of Bulgaria. One of his advisers suggested a tour of the European courts, and Alexander agreed. He had been recommended to make the acquaintance of a princess of Weimar, whom he called 'old and ugly', but as for the daughter of the Crown Prince and Princess of Prussia, he said, 'I shall probably see her in the spring, then I might speak to her about it.'[1] These were hardly the words of a besotted suitor, but Alexander was a young ruler who knew where his dynastic obligations lay.

During the Russo-Turkish War of 1877-78, Alexander had volunteered for service in the Russian army. He was encouraged to do so by his father, who recognised that Tsar Alexander II was favourably disposed towards the family and that such a gesture might be generously repaid in years to come. Having fought with distinction in the war, Alexander was granted his opportunity once peace was declared. At the Congress of Berlin, the status of northern Bulgaria was raised to that of a principality, and a prince was required as its ruler. Alexander's military prowess, family connections, and his father's canvassing of the Congress, all worked to his advantage; in 1879, at the age of twenty-two, he was proclaimed Prince of the new sovereign territory.

Faced with corruption and intriguing envoys from Russia, Alexander's task was never going to be an easy one, and it was made worse in 1881 when his great supporter, Tsar Alexander II, was assassinated. The Tsar's eldest surviving son and successor, Tsar Alexander III, was in many ways very different from his father. He openly disliked the Battenberg family, of which Alexander was a member, and regarded the young ruler of Bulgaria with a feeling bordering on contempt.

Prince Alexander visited Berlin in the summer of 1882, and it was on this occasion, while paying his respects to the Crown Prince and Princess, that he first met Victoria. She was sixteen at the time, but very young and immature for her age. To Lady Ponsonby, a close friend of the royal family and wife of Queen Victoria's private secretary Sir Henry, she was 'a kind of wild, Scandinavian woman, with much of her mother's impetuosity and her eldest brother's eccentricity'.[2] As Lady Ponsonby observed, the Crown Princess, Wilhelm, and Victoria were all noted for their impulsive characters. Although Victoria seemed enchanted with her parents' handsome guest, Alexander did not give her serious consideration as a possible bride at this time.[3] However, on his return to the city in the spring of 1883, he was accorded a warm welcome by the Crown Princess, and her second daughter was led to believe that this would be the handsome young husband of whom she had dreamed. Whether Alexander was genuinely in love with her, or whether he merely regarded the eldest unmarried daughter of the next German Kaiser as a suitable wife, is open to doubt. Yet there is little doubt that Victoria had fallen for him. Her mother and Queen Victoria both sanctioned the match, and they believed that both young people were made for each other.

While the course of events is unclear, it seems that before Alexander left Berlin, he and Victoria had come to an informal agreement that would presumably lead to an engagement if all parties, including senior members of the imperial family, were willing. However, those who were most closely involved, particularly the chancellor, were well aware that the match would be viewed by the courts of St Petersburg and Berlin as unfriendly towards the Tsar; it was even kept a secret from Alexander's father, Prince Alexander of Hesse.[4] The relations between Bismarck and Kaiser Wilhelm were strained, Princess Victoria was only aged seventeen and thought too young (even though the Crown Princess, then Victoria, Princess Royal of England, had been betrothed before her fifteenth birthday), and Alexander's position as Prince of Bulgaria was still regarded as uncertain.[5] It was a match the Crown Prince and Princess did not dare announce publicly.

Alexander broke the news to his father about a year later, at the marriage of his brother Louis to Victoria of Hesse at Darmstadt in April 1884. He told him that it was done with the full blessing of the princess's mother, but it was contrary to the wish of Kaiser Wilhelm. The Empress Augusta, even more hostile to the match, told her husband to write to the Crown Prince saying that as long as he lived, a Hohenzollern princess would never marry a Battenberg. To give approval to such a marriage would anger Tsar Alexander III and place an intolerable strain on the Russo-German friendship. Meanwhile the Russian government was letting it be known through the embassies in Berlin, Vienna, and elsewhere that the Prince of Bulgaria was deeply in debt and keeping dubious company in his palace at Sofia. If he was serious about maintaining his position in Bulgaria, he could only do so under Russian protection, and this would only be possible if he agreed never to oppose any of the Tsar's policies.

The only people really in favour were the Crown Princess and her mother, and the former tried to persuade her husband that their daughter's happiness depended on such a marriage. To the great annoyance of the Crown Princess, her elder children were all strongly hostile to the idea. Heinrich and Charlotte were very disparaging, while Wilhelm bombastically threatened that he would personally 'club the Battenberger to death' if he persisted in even daring to consider such a match, and he also said he would break off relations with his parents altogether if the marriage did come to pass.

In a discussion with Bismarck's son Herbert, he wondered aloud whether the best way of dealing with his sister's inappropriate suitor might be 'to provoke him to a duel and put a bullet through his head'.[6] When he came to write his memoirs some forty years later, he remarked more benignly (and none too convincingly) that as a kindly elder brother he 'took the personal fate' of his sister very much to heart, 'but as the well-being of the Fatherland was at stake, all personal desires had to be silenced'.[7] Wilhelm's wife, Augusta Victoria, known in the family as 'Dona', also looked down on the Battenbergs as being unworthy. In her case there was a whiff of hypocrisy, as Queen Victoria would later point out, as she had been born a princess of the house of Schleswig-Holstein-Sonderburg-Augustenburg. Although undeniably aristocratic themselves, the Augustenburgs, like the Battenbergs, were of somewhat less royal blood than the Hohenzollerns. Victoria was in despair, the Crown Princess wrote to her mother in August 1883, saying that she was always afraid 'that he will meet some Princess whom he will like better. Do you think he can wait?'[8]

Within a few months, the Crown Princess had greater grounds for optimism. By the spring of 1884, she thought, the prince's position in Bulgaria would be sufficiently secure for him to withstand any Russian attempt to overthrow him. She imagined that the Crown Prince, who adored his daughter, would surely relent, despite his reservations about Alexander's ancestry and the Tsar's attitude towards him; and she also hoped that the Kaiser, having expressed a personal liking for Alexander, would also give the engagement his support.[9]

Alexander was clearly being encouraged to do more than wait for his princess. During the early months of 1884 it became increasingly apparent that Bismarck would not do anything to offend Russia, and by August, Alexander was reporting to his father that the Crown Princess had advised him, via his brother Louis, that it might be necessary for him to abdicate from the Bulgarian throne in order to ensure the marriage. He wrote that he would do so with the greatest possible pleasure if he could still marry her. If another Battenberg brother, Heinrich, married Queen Victoria's youngest daughter Beatrice, which looked very likely at the time, Alexander thought the Kaiser would finally give his consent. He was sure that Victoria would 'stick' to him, and he had heard from Berlin that the Kaiser believed she would 'get her way after all'. Regarding the Crown Princess's suggestion of his abdication, Alexander wrote that it was 'the happiest possible means for me to get out of this wretched Bulgaria with a whole skin'.[10] Any official opposition from her parents-in-law and Bismarck only made the Crown Princess more determined to see the marriage through, especially as it was supported by Queen Victoria, who regarded her hopes to marry Alexander to her daughter with affectionate interest. On Christmas Eve 1884, the eighteen-year-old Princess Victoria wrote to her grandmother from Berlin, thanking her for the comfort and support she had been providing:

> This is the first Xmas I spend melancholy. My thoughts are not here tonight but far away where they always are. You know where, dearest Grandmama. Oh, if I can but only get a glimpse of him, so low in spirits am I, and there seems no hope. If beloved Mama were not there to rouse me up perpetually I don't know what would become of me.[11]

Ironically, it was at around this time that the prospect of a marriage between the Hohenzollerns and the Romanovs was being canvassed. In November 1883 the Russian foreign minister, Nikolai de Giers, arrived in Berlin for discussions to improve relations between both empires. They resulted in Bismarck agreeing to give Russia a free hand in Bulgaria. A few months later, Bismarck's son Herbert, who was working at the German Embassy in St Petersburg, suggested that a Russo-German alliance would be facilitated if a marriage was arranged between Princess Sophie and Grand Duke Nicholas, the Tsarevich, son and heir of Tsar Alexander III. As she was aged only fourteen at the time and the Tsarevich was just two years older, any marriage would have been some years ahead. The idea was never pursued, but in view of the Tsar's attitude towards the Prince of Bulgaria, the Crown Princess would certainly not have looked kindly on the suggestion, regardless of what her husband and father-in-law might have thought.

By new year's day 1885, some of the delegates to the National Assembly in Bulgaria had noticed that, since his return from Germany, Alexander wore a gold bracelet; they believed this to be a sign of his engagement to Victoria. But the Austro-Hungarian minister, Baron Ludwig von Biegeleben, reported to the diplomat Count Gustav Kálnoky that the prince was becoming despondent about his prospects; he felt that as a private individual he would have had a far better marriage than what he could expect in his present position, 'on such an insecure throne, as semi-suzerain of a remote, inhospitable and half-civilized country'.[12] A few years previously, Alexander had hoped he might become engaged to his old childhood friend Princess Beatrice, and now he stressed that he had never asked for the hand of Princess Victoria of Prussia. The suggestion, he said, had come from the Crown Princess, after they had 'both been attracted to each other' at the wedding of Louis to Victoria of Hesse the previous year, but it came to nothing as the German Kaiser refused to give his consent. He believed that the Kaiser would have consented had it not been for the influence of Empress Augusta, who was strongly against an alliance between a Hohenzollern and a Battenberg on the grounds of inequality of rank. Biegebelen gained the impression that although the prince regarded the situation as almost hopeless, he had been encouraged to wait 'until a more favourable opportunity presents itself'. [13]

Queen Victoria's partisanship of the Battenbergs was not only strengthened by the marriage of Louis and Victoria, but also by the betrothal of Heinrich and Beatrice early in the year, followed by their wedding in July 1885. Caught in a difficult position, the Crown Prince stopped short of forbidding his daughter to become betrothed to Prince Alexander, but he was well aware that it could not take place with his parents and Bismarck so strongly against it. He was still reluctant to give it his full blessing as, like Empress Augusta, he did not consider a Battenberg, born of a morganatic marriage, sufficiently royal for his daughter. Queen Victoria was particularly annoyed when he spoke of Alexander's brother Heinrich 'as not being of *Geblut* (stock), a little like animals'.[14]

By now the Crown Princess had outwardly relented that the marriage was impossible, given the implacable opposition of the Kaiser, the Empress, Bismarck, and Prince Wilhelm. However, she did not entirely give up hope. She was relying to a certain extent on Sir Howard Elphinstone, who had been appointed as an attaché at the British Embassy in Berlin the previous year, and whose duties thus included that of confidential adviser to Queen Victoria. The Crown Princess feared that Bismarck's spies would intercept highly confidential letters to the Prince of Bulgaria in Sofia, so she began to use Elphinstone as an unofficial courier to send messages to Alexander from herself and Victoria. She insisted that they could not entrust any confidential correspondence to the post. 'Could it not go as a letter from you to the English minister at Sofia or is it not safe,' she wrote to Elphinstone in January 1885. 'I wonder whether they watch what letters you write at your hotel?'[15]

She was aware that she had long been surrounded by spies on all sides—'until one knows that a letter is safe one feels in a perfect fever,' she wrote. If the letters had been discovered, the scandal would have done considerable harm to her reputation, but as she knew that among sections of the Berlin court her name counted for little anyway, she was probably prepared to take the risk. The system helped her and Victoria keep in touch with Alexander, but while the main powers in Berlin were determined that the marriage could never be, it must have seemed a lost cause. Yet she was always relieved to know that the letters had reached their destination without being intercepted or read by prying eyes. 'I cannot tell you the infinite relief it was to get your letter and the enclosed, which did bring one little ray of sunshine and of HOPE, though it is but faint,' she wrote to Elphinstone later that year. 'Still it took a load off my mind. This I owe to you, or I should never have had it! You would have been repaid if you had seen my poor child's tears of gratitude!'[16]

The Prince of Bulgaria was increasingly unhappy with the controversy the mere idea of any engagement had generated. He was acutely conscious that the matter of one of his brothers marrying into the British royal family and with a second shortly to do likewise had done nothing to advance his cause with the three people whose views mattered most, namely Kaiser Wilhelm, Empress Augusta, and Bismarck. 'God knows how it will all end,' he wrote sadly to his father in February 1885. 'I have already done too much harm in my life. Things have always ended badly for anyone who loved me. I should feel like a criminal if I started on any fresh marriage project. Until Vicky marries I am not free.'[17]

For about a year, letters passed between the Crown Princess and Elphinstone. In November 1885, Serbia, backed by Austria-Hungary, invaded Bulgaria, but under the leadership of Alexander the Serbian army was driven back at the battle of Slivitzna. In April 1886, the Great Powers—Great Britain, France, Germany, Russia, and Austria-Hungary—accepted the union of Bulgaria and Eastern Roumelia. The Crown Princess and Victoria were full of admiration for Alexander, but at this point, Bismarck suggested that the twenty-year-old princess ought to consider marrying Prince Carlos, heir to the throne of Portugal, a move which would have meant her changing her religion and becoming a Roman Catholic. However, she did not care for Prince Carlos, and the fact that the suggestion came from Bismarck can hardly have endeared her to the idea anyway. Bismarck responded by asking the Kaiser to forbid the Crown Princess to take Victoria on a visit to her grandmother, where she would be able to meet Alexander's brothers Louis and Heinrich.

By this time, Alexander's position was becoming increasingly tenuous. The popularity in Bulgaria that he had won after his victory the previous year was strongly resented at St Petersburg, and only one thing might save his position—immediate marriage to a suitable princess. Before he had a chance to make further overtures to Victoria, on the night of 20/21 August a gang of Russian officers broke into his palace at Sofia, forced him at gunpoint to sign a hastily improvised deed of abdication, and sent him under arrest to the Austrian frontier. After an emotional reunion with his brother Louis, they decided that the only means of salvation for Bulgaria lay in a reconciliation with the Tsar, and that a telegram to him on the subject would be the right approach. They accordingly drafted one in which Alexander said that he wished to give His Majesty proof of his 'unchanging devotion', and as Russia had given him his crown, 'I am prepared to give it back into the hands of its Sovereign'.[18] The Tsar wrote him a brief reply in acknowledgement, and then released the text of his reply, plus Alexander's telegram. Only then did the latter realise what a mistake he had made. Queen Victoria and his father were both aghast, his father in particular, telling him that it was a political error which would be exploited to his disadvantage throughout Europe: 'you have cast your pearls before swine'.[19]

Public opinion in Bulgaria was already demanding his immediate return, but he had had enough. The sovereign state over which he had been chosen to rule was a poisoned chalice, and he wanted nothing more to do with it. Despite this, Victoria was encouraged by her mother to believe that although Alexander was no longer a ruling prince, there would be no obstacles to their marriage. The Crown Princess was convinced that when her husband came to the throne, she would be able to persuade him to agree; they just had to bide their time until Kaiser Wilhelm, now aged almost ninety and increasingly feeble after several minor strokes, was in his grave. Dr Karl Langenbuch, a physician at the Berlin court who was on close terms with the Crown Prince and Princess, reported that the elderly Kaiser had told Bismarck that if the Prince of Bulgaria was to come to Berlin, 'I shall no longer refuse him my granddaughter Victoria'. He said the Kaiser wanted to put an end to the misery his refusal was causing, and that Bismarck had agreed.[20] However, nothing was confirmed and the story was thought to be no more than a rumour.

In reality, by this time Alexander had had enough. In December 1886 he wrote to Queen Victoria stating that although he had never formally asked for the Princess's hand (which rather gives credence to assertions of a secret engagement three years earlier), he had been repeatedly insulted by 'remonstrances' and attempts to ward him off. It was therefore impossible for him to 'make any fresh advances,' stating plainly that 'if anything is to come of the affair, Friedrich Wilhelm of Prussia must take the first step.' The Queen warned the Crown Princess not to approach Alexander on the matter again, until it was certain that he would be received with the respect and cordiality he had the right to expect. He did not want 'any secret or underhand dealings,' she concluded, for these had 'already brought him much undeserved sorrow.'[21]

By the spring of 1887, Crown Prince Friedrich Wilhelm was also unwell. For years he had suffered from heavy colds during the winter months and depression, brought on by his fears that the succession would skip a generation. When he consulted his physicians after a bout of illness lasting throughout the autumn and winter, which he seemed unable to shake off, and a bad throat which had left him so hoarse that he could barely speak, a medical examination revealed a small swelling on the left vocal cord. Efforts to remove it proved unsuccessful, and what was initially thought to be a simple tumour was diagnosed as a cancerous growth.

The Crown Princess was increasingly worried that this illness would prove fatal. She still hoped that Victoria would be able to marry Alexander one day, though he was now a private citizen of no political importance, with not the slightest intention of returning to the territory from which his enforced exit had left him a broken man. The members of the family who had always opposed the idea of the marriage, notably Victoria's elder siblings and her grandparents in Berlin, continued to do so, with the ageing but still indomitable Empress Augusta particularly clamorous. With the help of her daughter Louise, Grand Duchess of Baden, the Empress prepared a codicil to the will of the Kaiser, who was now in poor health and thought to be dying. It stated that if she married the former Prince of Bulgaria, she and her mother, the Crown Princess, would both be disinherited and would therefore receive nothing.

The three princesses were their parents' devoted companions through these anxious months. In June 1887, the Crown Prince and Princess attended the Golden Jubilee celebrations for Queen Victoria, and while they were in England, Sophie met Constantine, Crown Prince of Greece, a nephew of the Princess of Wales, for the first time. The burgeoning romance was inevitably watched with interest by those closest to them.

Victoria, Sophie, and Margaret accompanied their parents to Balmoral after the Jubilee festivities at London and Windsor. At the end of the summer they all moved to San Remo, where the Crown Prince had been advised to spend the next few months to avoid Berlin's bitter winter. While they were there, Alexander wrote to the Crown Princess to say that although he loved Princess Victoria, circumstances forced him 'to request her to dispose of her daughter's hand without any regard to himself'.[22]

When Kaiser Wilhelm died at the age of ninety on 9 March 1888, it had been apparent for some weeks that his son, now Kaiser Friedrich III, was himself a dying man. It would not have surprised some observers if he had predeceased his father. He had already been diagnosed with cancer of the larynx, and in February he had undergone a tracheotomy which involved fitting a tube into his throat to prevent suffocation. However, the operation left him unable to speak, and the only way he could communicate was by writing everything he needed to say down on a pad of paper.

After the family's return to Berlin, Victoria recorded in her memoirs that at Potsdam her father gave her his consent personally to her betrothal with the former Prince of Bulgaria, 'and how lovingly we embraced one another'.[23] It was suggested that the Empress intended to invite Alexander to Berlin forthwith, offer him a senior post in the German army—for which the victor of Slivitzna would have been well suited—and proceed with the marriage without delay. Bismarck, who may well have been responsible for this story, threatened to resign as imperial chancellor over the issue. He claimed that if the marriage took place, all that he had achieved with Tsar Alexander III would be lost, that Russia would ally herself with France, and that in the event of a European war, even if it ended in German victory, it would prove to be a disaster for the empire.

He also let it be known that he feared the Empress planned to dismiss him and make the former Prince of Bulgaria imperial chancellor in his place, though this scheme was too farfetched to be at all plausible. Nevertheless, her brother-in-law Louis, Grand Duke of Hesse and the Rhine, also wrote to the Empress personally, urging her to abandon any ideas of the marriage in view of the probable consequences. At the same time Alexander wrote to the Grand Duke, saying that he failed to see how the marriage could be interpreted as a threat to Russia, now that he was a figure of no political importance and had no intention of returning to Bulgaria. He also wrote to the Empress, saying he did not want to be seen by the German people as the man who had been responsible for the downfall or resignation of Bismarck, or as one who was in the pay of England and had destroyed the German empire.[24]

On 12 April the Empress persuaded her husband, in adding a codicil to his will, to exhort his eldest son when he became Kaiser to allow the marriage to take place. She still hoped that a wedding could be held at Homburg in May, or, should the Kaiser die first, a private ceremony would be staged in England, although this would mean an acceptance by the young couple of their banishment from the Kingdom of Prussia.[25]

In private conversation, Bismarck was quite unrestrained on the subject of the Empress and the former sovereign prince, declaring that she was completely besotted with him. In conversation with his friend Baroness Hildegard von Spitzemberg, wife of the Württemberg ambassador to Berlin, he said that she was 'a wild woman', who 'terrified him [Bismarck] by the unrestrained sexuality which speaks through her eyes'. She had 'fallen in love with the Battenberger and wants him near her, and like her mother, whom the English call "the selfish old beast", holds onto her brothers, with who knows what sort of incestuous thoughts.'[26]

However, his chances of seeing the problem solve itself were greatly strengthened when he learned that Alexander was cooling over the idea of the marriage. His humiliation at the hands of the Russians had broken his health and spirits, and since leaving Bulgaria he had fallen in love with an opera singer, Joanna Loisinger, whom he had first seen perform in the state theatre at Hesse and then met in person not long after his enforced departure from Bulgaria. When the Empress wrote to him with the news that she intended to ask her husband to settle his marriage, he quickly wrote back to say that as his circumstances, position, and situation were now very different, the prospects for their happiness were very slight. Queen Victoria urged her daughter not to proceed with any marriage plans, her main reason being that it would be folly without first coming to an understanding with her son, now Crown Prince Wilhelm.

As the Queen made no mention of Fraülein Loisinger, it seems possible that she was unaware of the lady's existence. However, it would seem strange if she had not already been told about her by either of Alexander's brothers, one of whom, Heinrich, was her son-in-law, who with his wife Beatrice and young family, lived with her. Other sources suggest that Bismarck himself had told her, but as he had been so unreliable and untrustworthy in the past, she thought he was lying. It was unfortunate that somebody more honest could not have been relied upon to give her the news. It is unknown at what exact point the Empress realised beyond doubt, and to her mortification, that Alexander now loved another woman, and one to whom there would be no obstacles regarding their marriage. Had she known, she would surely have blamed herself bitterly for giving her daughter false hope, but there is no mention of Fraülein Loisinger in any surviving correspondence, and it appears that she was unaware of any rival for Alexander's hand during the last few weeks of her husband's life.

On 24 April, Queen Victoria arrived in Berlin to come and pay what she knew would be a final visit to her dying son-in-law. The time she and Empress Victoria were able to spend alone was limited, but during a brief *tête-a-tête*, in which the younger woman wept a great deal, the Queen spoke of the betrothal, told her daughter that it had gone on too long, and the time had come to let it go. The following day she had a conversation with Bismarck, which he had been dreading, as he thought she would take the opportunity to insist that the betrothal and marriage of her granddaughter should take place. She left an account of what proved to be a perfectly amicable meeting in her journal, in which she alluded to various 'personal' matters, one of them probably being her agreement that she too regarded the scheme as impracticable. After it was finished, the nervous imperial chancellor came out mopping his brow, muttering in amazement, 'That was a woman! One could do business with her!'[27]

The family took encouragement from every little sign of improvement in the Kaiser's condition, as is clear from a letter from Victoria to Mrs Talbot, a family friend in London, written from Charlottenburg Palace on 5 April:

> We have again been through days of much anxiety—Papa having been so ill—now, thank God, the doctors are more satisfied & we are all feeling happier with the present state of things—it is terrible to see those one loves suffer & not be able to help—one cannot understand why just beloved Papa should have to endure such a lot—he who is goodness & kindness itself—but still I am full of hope & with Heaven's help there may be better times in store for us![28]

Yet any hopes of a lasting improvement would prove illusory, as did any prospect of Victoria's marriage to Alexander. Although she does not seem to have alluded to it in her letters, even the Empress, redoubtable optimist though she might appear, had almost certainly come to accept with sadness that it would never happen. Yet, of even greater worry to her was the question of what would become of her and her daughters after the inevitable occurred. For the Kaiser, who could no longer speak above a whisper and was constantly wracked with pain, the end was not far off.

At the beginning of June, Kaiser Friedrich, the Empress and their daughters went by river to the Neue Palais, Potsdam, which had been their summer home throughout their married life. As they came towards the end of their journey, the Kaiser wrote a note saying that he would like the palace to be renamed 'Friedrichskron'.

On the morning of Sophie's eighteenth birthday, 14 June, the Kaiser insisted that the family ought to have a boating trip to the Pfaueninsel, the island in the River Havel. At nine o'clock in the morning, when all three sisters came over together, he embraced Sophie and handed her the bouquet he had ordered as her present. Needless to say, he was so ill that he could not be moved, and there was no prospect of them going out anywhere. That night he was very restless, constantly changing his position and coughing a great deal. Next morning, after a reign of just ninety-nine days, during which he had been little more than a voiceless figurehead, he slipped into unconsciousness and died, aged fifty-six.

All his children had been warned that he could not live for more than a day or two, and each one was present at his deathbed. The three younger sisters were horrified to witness at first hand the brutal treatment meted out to their mother during the next few days. Troops surrounded the Neue Palais, which had reverted to its old name in one of the first acts of the new Kaiser Wilhelm II. Rooms and desks were searched for any private correspondence of the newly widowed Empress, but she had had the foresight to remove it all. A post-mortem and funeral were arranged, both without her consent.

Accompanied by her three younger daughters, the Empress Frederick, as she would now be known for the rest of her life, fled to her farmhouse at Bornstadt. She knew that her daughters would now rely on her for support more than ever. 'I have my three sweet girls—whom he [Friedrich] loved so much—that are my consolation,'[29] she wrote to Queen Victoria. Although she deliberately avoided all controversy when she came to write her memoirs nearly forty years later, Victoria had to admit that the weeks following her father's death were indeed a time of bitterness and sorrow. Their grandmother summed up the general state of affairs all too well: 'It is too dreadful for us all to think of Willy & Bismarck & Dona—being the supreme head of all now! Two so unfit & one so wicked.'[30]

A few days after his accession, Kaiser Wilhelm was handed the letter from his father by the Prussian Minister for Justice, Heinrich von Friedberg, asking him to give his assent to the marriage between his sister and Alexander of Battenberg. Friedberg said that the letter was legally invalid as the Kaiser had signed it at the instigation of his wife and at a time when he was not in full possession of his faculties. The Kaiser repeated that he would never agree to the marriage, and wrote to Prince Alexander, demanding that he should make a solemn renunciation of the hand of Princess Victoria to him as Kaiser and head of the family. The prince replied that he could not answer the letter before he had seen the text of the late Kaiser's will. Irritated, Kaiser Wilhelm said he would not write another letter, but would have his intentions communicated verbally. Alexander of Hesse then wrote to the Kaiser to say that on his orders, his son had broken off the engagement, and would like to know whether his son might hope for some post in the army. To his fury, if perhaps not to his surprise, the letter was returned to him unopened.

The former Prince of Bulgaria wrote a letter of condolence to the Empress and her daughter, saying that although he was 'still true' to the latter, he was deeply wounded, and could only attribute the new Kaiser's letter to the fact that when it was written, Kaiser Friedrich's will had not been published. He said he was writing to Kaiser Wilhelm that the Empress Frederick had informed him of the will, and in her letter she had referred to Princess Victoria as 'the bride of Prince Alexander to whom her dying father had entrusted her'.[31] Baron Thielmann, the Prussian Minister in Darmstadt, told Alexander that he had had instructions to inform him that His Majesty had received his letter, and that it gave him no grounds for any addition to the Kaiser's previous communication. Because of political and family considerations, he was not in a position to agree to the marriage, and the matter must be regarded as closed.

On receiving this, Alexander shut himself away in his rooms at Darmstadt, refused to let anybody else in, and packed up all the gifts he had received from Victoria so they would be ready to return to her. Behind locked doors, he wrote to Joanna Loisinger, 'I have allowed my tears to flow without being able to prevent it; they were for the grave of my youthful dreams, the collapse of all for which I had striven and hoped for thirty years, the failure of all my military plans.' He then wrote final farewell letters to the Empress and her daughter, explaining that the late Kaiser Friedrich had the chance to bring him and Princess Victoria together but had not done so because he did not wish to, 'and had given its fulfilment into the hands of one who would never carry it out,' namely the present Kaiser. There was no point in waiting any longer, so he was renouncing the dreams of his youth and saying farewell to his fiancée with tender words. In view of Kaiser Wilhelm's attitude, it would be impossible for him to continue the correspondence any further.[32]

As the sun set firmly on one romance in the family, it rose on another. One month later, Sophie's future was beginning to occupy the minds of her mother and grandmother. 'Is there a chance of Sophie's marrying Tino of Greece?' Queen Victoria suggested. 'It would be very nice for her, for he is very good.'[33] 'Tino' was the twenty-year-old Duke of Sparta, Crown Prince Constantine of Greece, the eldest son of King George. Unlike the thwarted affair of her elder sister, Sophie's matrimonial future proceeded without any complications. An alliance of this nature with the Greek royal family fitted in well with the hopes and aspirations of Kaiser Wilhelm and Bismarck. On 3 September the Kaiser informed his mother that the Crown Prince of Greece had asked him as head of the family for the hand of his sister in marriage. The future of Greece and her relations with her neighbours in the Balkans did not look harmonious, and this was one of the reasons for the Empress's misgivings. Nevertheless she was very pleased for her daughter's sake. 'If only the bridegroom were not so young,' she noted in her diary, 'and Greece so far away and one of the elements in the unsolved and dangerous eastern question! He is very nice and charming and well brought up.'[34]

Queen Victoria had no such reservations, as she made clear in a letter to the Empress the next day:

> ... let me wish you joy (though I ought not to say that for I can never feel it) and satisfaction over dear Sophie's engagement. Tino is a good, steady young man and Sophie likes him very much and he comes from, and belongs to, loving parents and a very united, loving family. And this is a priceless blessing. A good heart and good character after all go far beyond great cleverness. Olga of Greece [Queen Olga, consort of King George] is a sweet, dear creature and will be kindness itself to Sophie.[35]

The impending good news about Sophie's engagement was one of the few happy moments in the life of the newly widowed Empress. For the first few weeks of her widowhood she shut herself away as far as possible from the outside world, relying mostly on her three younger daughters and the recently widowed Frau von Stockmar, whose father-in-law had been a close family friend and adviser to Queen Victoria and Prince Albert during their first years of married life. Attacked and persecuted in the pro-government press and cold-shouldered by her eldest son, she suffered from severe depression, neuralgia, and rheumatism. 'Oh God, why was I not allowed to go with him—why, oh why this separation?' she wrote in despair to her mother three days after her husband died. '... More cruel suffering was never laid on human soul than on mine at this moment!'[36]

After all the stress and misery she had been through during the last few months, she could not wait to return to England for a long overdue visit to her mother and family, and a much-needed rest from the oppressive atmosphere of Berlin. The British Prime Minister Lord Salisbury had suggested that it was too soon for her to leave Germany after Kaiser Friedrich's death, and that it risked undermining Anglo-German relations. But the Queen retorted that it would be 'impossible, heartless and cruel' to prevent her daughter and family from coming, and to do so would only encourage Kaiser Wilhelm and the Bismarcks (the Chancellor and his son Herbert, a senior Prussian minister) in their disgraceful behaviour towards her.[37]

While the Empress Frederick was making plans to return to England, the flame which the former Prince of Bulgaria had lit in the heart of Victoria of Prussia flickered for the last time. On 5 November the Kaiser accused his mother of having arranged to meet Alexander at the Frankfurt railway station. The following day, Victoria made one last appeal to her elder brother to allow her to marry the prince, and he refused. Although the Empress had almost certainly given up hope for the marriage, she seemed determined to support her daughter if this was still her dearest wish, in which case she must still have believed that the relations between Alexander and Joanna Loisinger amounted to nothing more than friendship. She wrote the Kaiser an angry letter, accusing him of 'heartless disregard' for his sister's feelings, and of repeatedly proving beyond doubt that his father's dying wishes carried no weight with him. She therefore intended to have no communication with him in future, 'beyond what is absolutely necessary'.[38]

On 19 November the Empress and her *Kleeblatt* arrived in England. Queen Victoria had sent the royal yacht *Victoria & Albert*, with the Prince of Wales and his second son George on board, to Flushing to meet them and accompany them on the crossing to Gravesend. As a rule the Queen never went further than her front door when welcoming even her most exalted guests to England, but this was no ordinary occasion, and her eldest daughter deserved nothing less than the best. The sovereign hoped that when the Kaiser heard of this reception, he would be shamed into treating her with more respect in future. She therefore made a special journey to Gravesend to meet the Empress, draped in crepe and trembling with grief, a thick black veil concealing the tears running down her face. When they landed, the princesses were just as overcome as their mother.

Mother and daughters went to Windsor to stay with Queen Victoria for the next three months. The Queen's granddaughter Princess Alice of Albany, who was then aged five, noted in her memoirs some seventy years later the arrival of her aunt Vicky, in black crepe, and her daughters all dressed in deepest mourning. 'What thrilled me was their red eyes, as they were all crying together—and Grandmama too. We gaped as may be imagined.' In spite of that, she noted, the three young sisters were charming to her and her four-year-old brother Charlie, 'and raced each other with Charlie and me pick-a-back on their bustles.'[39] There was, however, further sadness in store for them all when they received the news that Alexander had assumed the title Count von Hartenau, joined the Austrian army, and married Joanna Loisinger in February 1889. To Queen Victoria, it was 'a sad thing—especially that he did it without saying one word to any of his Brothers & in such a hurry!'[40]

Soon after they returned to Germany, preparations began for Sophie's wedding. Much as Victoria loved her sister, the wedding arrangements only added to her sense of depression and insecurity. In addition to her failed romance, the death of their father, their mother's grief, and the cruelty of her elder brother the Kaiser, Victoria was convinced that any hopes of marriage for her were disappearing. She began to diet and exercise fanatically, in an attempt to banish fears that she was too ugly and too old to attract a suitable partner. These feelings were compounded when Prince Karl of Sweden refused to consider her as a prospective bride. The Empress feared that her romantically minded but unlucky daughter might lose her heart to somebody of insufficient rank. Therefore, when Queen Victoria suggested that Grand Duke Alexander Michaelovich of Russia, whom she had met in London in May 1889, might be a suitable match, the Empress was eager to consider it. Grand Duke Alexander was the same age as Victoria, and was said to be a very charming young man who would undoubtedly appeal to them. He also had the advantage of speaking English perfectly.

While the Empress began her investigations, she sent Victoria on a short visit to her grandmother in England, feeling she needed a change of scene. Victoria arrived at Windsor in June 1889, carrying a letter from her mother to the Queen, in which the Empress outlined her hopes for her daughter's future and her worry over her general health and state of mind. The Empress begged her mother to try to induce Moretta

not to be so foolish about her food. Her one craze is to be thin! She starves completely, touches no milk, no sugar, no bread, no sweets, no soup, no butter, nothing but a scrap of meat & apples which is not enough. She will ruin her health. She has a fine strong constitution. She goes to bed too late and takes almost too much exercise. I have begged & prayed, ordered, threatened, all to no effect. She is quite fanatical on the subject.   Her pretty figure is quite spoilt from being too thin.[41]

In case her plans for a Hohenzollern-Romanov marriage fell through, the Empress was determined to find at least one or two other eligible bachelors who might prove to be a satisfactory husband for her daughter. Now aged twenty-three, Princess Victoria was of an age when she should have been a wife. If she had been heartbroken at the loss of Alexander—which is open to doubt—she had got over it quickly enough. She was a lively, outgoing young woman with a keen eye for good-looking young men; her mother feared that she might become attached to somebody ineligible or, worse still, become involved in a relationship which could end in scandal. Above all, she knew that the headstrong Kaiser would not think twice about disinheriting his sister altogether if she did anything to bring shame on the Hohenzollern dynasty. A suitable marriage was the only possible protection against such an unhappy occurrence.

While Victoria was at Windsor, the Empress went to meet Prince Adolf of Schaumburg-Lippe with a view to appraising him as a potential son-in-law. She kept the rendezvous secret from everybody except her mother, in order not to raise any false hopes which might be speedily dashed before long. She begged her mother not to tell Victoria. Writing to the Queen in May 1889, she described him as 'nice and good looking, but of course, it is nothing as to position'. At the same time, she gave some consideration to Prince Eduard of Anhalt, 'a nice good young man with a nice fortune and not ill-looking, who would be sure to make a kind, nice husband and who has an amiable and cheerful disposition and is a favourite everywhere'.[42] Another young candidate for Victoria's hand was Prince Albrecht of Württemberg, but he was considered less suitable as he was a Roman Catholic. This would later seem ironic in view of a bitter quarrel about religion which was to create even more ill-feeling in the family some eighteen months thereafter.

Outwardly, Victoria seemed to enjoy her few weeks in England. She spent much of her time walking, riding, and playing tennis, and also rehearsing for an amateur household theatrical performance. Yet her low spirits came through in the letters she sent regularly to her mother. She longed to be a wife and mother herself, and took pleasure with perhaps a pang of regret in helping to nurse Prince Leopold of Battenberg, the baby son of her aunt Princess Beatrice, writing in very affectionate terms of the child to her mother: 'You would enjoy it, & nibble at it—heaps of hair on its little head and a good pair of lungs.'[43]

The news of the engagement of Princess Louise, eldest daughter of the Prince of Wales, to the Earl of Fife, and that of the marriage of Grand Duke Paul of Russia to Princess Alexandra of Greece, added to Victoria's misery and intense feelings of rejection. It coincided with her learning that Grand Duke Alexander Michaelovich had no wish to become involved with her.

The Empress had thought that if her second daughter married into the Romanov dynasty and settled in Russia she might be a companion for her Hessian cousin Ella, the wife of Grand Duke Sergei Alexandrovich, one of the younger brothers of Tsar Alexander III. The Tsar's part in Alexander's enforced abdication and departure from Bulgaria seems to have counted for strangely little in the Empress's plans, or perhaps this was a sign of her desperation at the thought that there were so few eligible bachelors available. Besides, Ella disliked Victoria, whom she regarded as 'a complete spoilt child', and had never forgiven her for what she saw as the 'ruin' of her cousin Alexander.[44] Yet at least, in future years, Victoria could look back on what might have been, and consider that she had had a lucky escape. Ella, who took holy orders after her husband was assassinated in 1905, also perished at the hands of the Bolsheviks when she was thrown down a mineshaft in the 1918 revolution; while Grand Duke Alexander, who married his cousin Xenia and was fortunate to escape the revolution with her, was prone to infidelity and separated from his wife.

Knowing that her eldest daughter's attitude in finding husbands for her daughters bordered on the obsessive, Queen Victoria told the Empress that it might be as well if they were to stop deliberately looking for someone. They had now had what she called 'three direct failures', and Moretta had 'expressed a strong wish not to marry now'. It was all very well to allow her to see other people, but she should not be forced or pressed to marry for the sake of marriage. 'I think it hardly right or dignified for you to go about trying to marry your daughter & getting refusals,' said the Queen.[45]

The following day Victoria wrote in despair to her mother, a self-pitying letter which to some extent mirrored her grandmother's advice. She insisted that she would never marry, as she was too ugly: 'All my relations, sisters, friends do [marry] except my stupid self, nobody will have me, nothing but disappointment is my lot in life.'[46] It was a *cri de coeur* from a miserable young woman, totally lacking in self-esteem, who, as her mother feared, would probably accept any bachelor prepared to consider her for a wife.

Yet the Empress found herself in a difficult position. That week she wrote to Queen Victoria, pointing out that she could not see 'the great difficulties and drawbacks of the existence of a young unmarried Princess who is no longer a child! especially at a court like the Berlin one.' She could not give Moretta the liberty and independence she would like, as 'everything is criticised, commented upon, & twisted' against them. Repugnant though it was for her to be seen making the acquaintance of young men who might be suitable for her daughter, the Empress felt obliged to make the effort to 'weigh what chances there might be for her.'[47]

3

'Serious and grave but no tears'
1889–93

Princess Victoria left Windsor on 1 July 1889 for Germany. By this time there was much speculation in the press concerning potential husbands for her, and within a few days, the newspapers were denying ill-founded rumours that an engagement was about to be announced between the princess and her cousin 'Eddy', Prince Albert Victor of Wales. Ironically it was the prince's father, the Prince of Wales, who made the first serious recommendation for his niece in Berlin; Prince Karl of Sweden, he told the Crown Princess, might make a suitable husband for her daughter. However, Karl's elder brother Gustav, the future King, had married Victoria's cousin, Princess Victoria of Baden, whose mother Louise was the only sister of the late Kaiser Friedrich. This Princess Victoria was an imperious young woman, who succeeded in completely putting her brother-in-law off any idea of taking a Hohenzollern princess as his bride.

Once Victoria had arrived back at home, she found her mother was increasingly involved in the final preparations for the wedding of Sophie and Constantine. As the day drew nearer, it became an increasingly painful reminder of what might have been in her case. She and the Empress Frederick sailed to Greece on board the yacht *Surprise*. One of the officers serving on board ship was Captain Maurice Bourke, son of the Earl of Mayo. After the journey it was rumoured that Victoria had become rather fond of the good-looking unmarried naval officer.

The wedding of Sophie and Constantine on 27 October 1889 was not only the first great international occasion in the history of modern Greece, but also a wedding which united five ruling European dynasties: those of Denmark, Britain, Russia, Germany, and Greece. Among the attendees were King Christian and Queen Louise of Denmark, the Prince and Princess of Wales, the Tsarevich—who, if others had had their way, might have married the bride himself—and Kaiser Wilhelm II, his brother

Heinrich, and all their sisters. The streets throughout Athens had been richly decorated with bunting and wreaths of laurel leaves, with words of welcome to the bride displayed on all the main buildings; while the roads from the palace to the cathedral were thronged with peasants, dressed in colourful traditional costumes. However, not every effort had been spared. When Kaiser Wilhelm arrived at Piraeus at the end of his voyage on board the yacht *Hohenzollern*, there was no welcoming party of Greek ships or organised reception, and King George and Queen Olga were not present to welcome him to their country. He took it as a personal slight and would never forget it.

The wedding itself was a suitably spectacular affair. Ablaze with jewels and orders, the royals drove in borrowed carriages through sunlit streets to the new Orthodox Cathedral. The Crown Prince's best men were his brothers George and Nicholas and the Tsarevich, while Sophie's bridesmen were her brother Heinrich and her British cousins, Albert Victor and George of Wales. The Empress Frederick designed the silver tulle and white satin gown which Sophie wore for the occasion, though her bridal veil had been inadvertently left in Germany and they had to purchase a plain tulle veil from a shop in Athens. To the Protestant members of the family, the long ceremony seemed very theatrical, with hundreds of flickering candles, incense, jewel-studded icons, and bearded, mitred bishops. Crowns were held high above the bridal couple, and each held a lighted taper as they walked three times round a table draped in gold cloth with a Bible on it. Several guests found it quite exhausting, but the bridal couple acquitted themselves well as they stood for over an hour without betraying any sign of fatigue.

As Sophie had not yet been converted to Orthodoxy, the ceremony in the cathedral was followed by a short, simple Protestant service in King George's private palace chapel, conducted by the King's own chaplain. A family lunch followed, after which the bride changed from her lavishly embroidered gown into a dress of white and gold. A more opulent formal dinner followed, and the day ended with a spectacular fireworks display, bathing the Parthenon in greens and reds.

After the festivities the couple settled in a little rented villa in Kifissia Road, near the palace, which had been chosen as their first home. The Empress Frederick thought it was 'a tiny place, smaller than Osborne Cottage (a good deal), but light and cheerful and comfortable—arranged like a little French villa.'[1]

The wedding was greeted with great enthusiasm by the people of Greece, who saw this marriage as another step towards the realisation of their country's destiny. At his birth, Crown Prince Constantine had been hailed as the successor to the last Emperor of Byzantium; by taking as his bride a Princess Sophie, whose name recalled the Church of St Sophia in Constantinople, they firmly believed that Greece would once again know greatness, and Constantinople would fall into Greek hands. Sophie's brother-in-law Nicholas thought that the Greek people felt that now they were nearing the realisation of 'the dream that lasted through the dark centuries of slavery, the dream that had saved their souls from despair'.[2] When Sophie appeared outside the cathedral on the arm of her husband, the crowds went wild with enthusiasm.

The Empress Frederick felt very sad at the breaking up of her trio, but she admitted she was very proud of her 'darling Sophie, [who] looked so sweet and grave and calm, my little lamb'.[3] The parting was likewise a wrench for Sophie, who wrote afterwards to her mother: 'I also miss you dreadfully, it seems too strange not to have you anywhere.'[4]

In March 1890 it was reported in the *North German Gazette*, somewhat ambiguously, that a betrothal was about to be announced between Princess Victoria of Prussia and Prince Albert of Saxe-Altenburg, a widower of forty-seven. At the same time it was noted cautiously that 'this rumour need not be received with absolute faith'.[5] It emerged that there was, indeed, no substance in it, and some thought that before long any bachelor or widower prince in Germany of marriageable age would sooner or later be spoken of as a potential husband for Victoria.

However, the search had to continue. In June, the Empress introduced her daughter to Prince Ernst of Hohenlohe-Langenburg. This likewise came to nothing, and a few years later he married another of Queen Victoria's granddaughters, Princess Alexandra of Edinburgh. That same month, mother and daughter paid a visit to the Princess of Wied at Segenhaus, where among the guests was Adolf, the fourth son of the reigning Prince of Schaumburg-Lippe, and a lieutenant in the Bonner Hussars. Writing to Sophie in Athens, the Empress found it hard to muster much enthusiasm about her prospective son-in-law. Adolf was 'not clever,' she considered, 'and I believe that he has learned but very little, as his parents gave him no opportunity, but he has the highest praise from those who know him as being most trustworthy and good, and having a high character.... I think one can call him good-looking, with an amiable expression. This is all I can say about him. Perhaps he and Vicky will fancy each other, perhaps not, we must wait and see.'[6]

Adolf may have been neither brilliant nor polished, but the Empress hoped Victoria might find some consolation in him after her previous disappointments and her fears of becoming an old maid. Also, for the Empress, any marriage was better than the chance of a scandal, which she feared became greater the longer her daughter remained without a husband. Within days of their first meeting, Adolf proposed to Victoria and she accepted him. In her memoirs, she would claim that it was a case of love at first sight.[7] The Empress was nearer the truth when she wrote to Queen Victoria that Moretta had accepted Adolf, 'in her depression and discouragement, feeling that the happiness she had hoped for is not to be hers....' Wilhelm, she added, 'wishes this marriage particularly'. The Empress herself had cried bitterly over the decision, but she had assured herself that the young man was 'thoroughly trustworthy and good and I am sure he will try and make her happy'.[8]

To Sophie, the Empress expressed her fervent hope that the marriage would be for Moretta's lasting happiness, 'and that she may be repaid in her married life for all the sorrow and bitter disappointments she has gone through.' Adolf, she thought, seemed 'a little stiff and shy and awkward,' but she was sure this would wear off when he had had a chance to mix more in society.[9]

Queen Victoria thought her daughter was being a little gloomy about what should have been cause for celebration. 'Why should she not be happy?' she wrote in her reply. Any English marriage, she pointed out, would not have been possible, and with regard to Adolf's rank and connections, there was no cause for complaint. She herself was 'so very thankful that the dear child has at last found a good husband and I am sure she will be a good and affectionate and dutiful wife and that the restlessness will cease.' She also added, tactfully, that it was fortunate that the Kaiser approved, 'as it will make it so much easier for you'.[10]

In fact, the Kaiser had already been considering Adolf as a future brother-in-law. Anxious to see his sister safely married before she became involved with another unsuitable bachelor, Wilhelm was advised that this prince from the house of Schaumburg-Lippe might be the one. With this in mind, he had sent one of his favourite courtiers, Count Philipp von Eulenburg, to meet him and find out more, especially regarding his financial position and private life. The secret report, which the Kaiser burned having read it, proved entirely satisfactory.

However, at least two or three members of the family harboured grave doubts that the wedding would take place. According to an exchange of correspondence between Charlotte of Saxe-Meiningen and her aunt Marie, Duchess of Edinburgh, even after her betrothal to Adolf, Victoria was still in love with Captain Bourke, whom she had met aboard the *Surprise* on her voyage to Greece. If Charlotte and Marie were to be believed, the Empress Frederick had tried to persuade Queen Victoria to give the match her blessing. The Queen, said Marie, having been 'completely bamboozled' by her eldest daughter, had a conversation with Moretta and gave her a good scolding. Moretta 'took it quite lightly' and assured her grandmother that she 'never took the episode' very seriously. The Queen then gained a very different impression after talking to the Empress, who told her that Moretta 'was still madly in love with the gallant Captain', would have followed him to the end of the world, and was broken-hearted when he broke it off. At this, the Queen reportedly wept, and said that had she known it before the betrothal to Adolf, she would have helped Moretta the best she could in realising her dream. The only thing which would have frightened her was 'that dreadful tyrant Wilhelm', who 'makes rows about anything'. Queen Victoria's mind was 'in a terrible state', and she pretended that Charlotte was responsible for creating mischief. The Empress Frederick had been 'downright wicked by destroying her mother's peace of mind and happiness at the successful betrothal between Moretta and a real Prince'. Marie admitted that she would not be surprised if the Empress would still try and let her daughter marry Captain Bourke, and she still did not feel confident that he would marry Moretta after all. Ever ready to pass on such stories about her family, Charlotte had given the Duchess of Edinburgh's letter to Empress Augusta Victoria to copy. The latter accordingly copied it for the benefit of her husband, adding a letter of her own in which she said that they could not be sure of Moretta until the wedding had taken place, and suggesting that he give 'Grandmama a good talking-to', as it was surely going too far when a princess who was engaged had her own mother trying to break it off.[11]

Readers must draw their own conclusions about the veracity of such gossip. But Charlotte was notorious for embellishing stories about her family, and she had always been on the best of terms with the Duchess of Edinburgh, a bitter woman who had never liked Queen Victoria or indeed most of her in-laws, and whose marriage to the hard-drinking Alfred had not been a happy one. If all she said was true, then that paints the Empress Frederick in a very harsh light, but otherwise one must assume that somebody was out to make mischief. After the years of unhappiness that mother and daughter had suffered—largely as a result of the thwarted romance with Alexander of Battenberg—it was extremely unlikely that the Empress would have allowed her daughter to consider a marriage which would surely have been opposed just as firmly by Kaiser Wilhelm. Some twenty years earlier Queen Victoria had allowed her fourth daughter Louise to marry a member of the Scottish aristocracy, and it is not unreasonable to assume that she would not have been averse to one of her granddaughters forming a similar alliance with an Irish aristocrat of unimpeachable character. Yet even if she had had any influence over the matter, she and her daughter would have known at once that the Kaiser would never have allowed it to happen.

Though it is likely that she, like her mother, was under no illusions about Adolf's unprepossessing manners and appearance, Victoria was soon caught up in preparations for her wedding. While she did not imagine that this would be an idyllic marriage, at least she had the prospect of a good, steady husband, a home of her own and the possibility of children. She also had the consolation, such as it was, of knowing that her eldest brother wholeheartedly approved of Adolf as a brother-in-law. On 17 June, Kaiser Wilhelm gave a grand luncheon at Potsdam for a hundred guests including his family and all the high officials of state. It was the occasion for an official announcement of the engagement. Victoria wore a cream-coloured dress and hat trimmed with white flowers, while Adolf was attired in the uniform of the Bonn Hussars. They sat between the Kaiser and Empress as everyone offered their congratulations.

In July Victoria and Adolf joined her sister Mossy and the Empress on a visit to Queen Victoria at Windsor, where she formally introduced Adolf to her grandmother. She approved of him, and if she had reservations, she kept them to herself. She liked Adolf but could see that her granddaughter was not altogether happy. She told Princess Louis of Battenberg that they liked him a great deal and that he was 'very good-looking, amiable & sensible. But of course she cannot feel the <u>same</u> as she did for Sandro. That was a <u>passion</u> & <u>1st</u> attachment. Still, I think, she will be happy & make a good wife. He is <u>very</u> fond of her.'[12] On their return to Germany the young couple made a visit to Buckeburg, so that Victoria could meet her future parents-in-law.

Meanwhile, in February 1890 the Crown Princess of Greece informed her mother that she was expecting a child. The Empress Frederick thought that her daughter might need some assistance in a city which was, by her standards, somewhat medically primitive, and she accordingly smuggled into Sophie's entourage a midwife from Germany. 'Of course I could not tell you what her real profession was when you were a young girl,' she wrote to Sophie, 'so I have to invent the name and function of housekeeper, so that you might have her always near at hand.'[13]

The Empress had also arranged to go to Greece and be with her daughter for the confinement, which was expected at the end of July or in early August. She travelled by sea on her mother's yacht *Victoria and Albert* with her two youngest daughters, accompanied by two nurses for the baby and the entire layette. Queen Victoria had cautioned her daughter not to 'mix the girls up in laying on unedifying and, for the future, alarming details', on the grounds that it might discourage the newly engaged Victoria from married life.[14] They had barely reached Gibraltar when news arrived that Sophie had given birth prematurely to a son on 19 July. It was a dangerous confinement; as with the Crown Princess's own first experience of childbirth, mother and son were in danger for a while. Had the German midwife not been present, it was quite possible that neither would have survived. Queen Olga arrived in Athens from a visit to Russia two days after the confinement, and the Empress visited at the end of July, bringing Victoria and Margaret, to see the infant prince who was christened George on 18 August. When she wrote to Queen Victoria about the birth of the new prince, describing the conditions in Athens, she begged her mother not to repeat any of it to Kaiser Wilhelm, as he disliked the Greek royal family and would only take it as another excuse for abusing them.

After the drama of Sophie's confinement, the family's attention turned once again to the forthcoming wedding of Victoria and Adolf. Whatever the truth was about an affair between Victoria and Captain Bourke, the bride-to-be did not seem to be looking forward to her forthcoming marriage, which had been arranged to take place on 19 November. During the late summer and early autumn, she was depressed and prone to bursting into tears. Although unfailingly sympathetic, the Empress was helpless to do anything other than offer reassurance. She wrote sadly to Queen Victoria in September that, 'the nearer the wedding approaches the more cast down she is'.[15]

Among the guests invited to the ceremony were the Empress's brother Alfred, Duke of Edinburgh (but apparently not the Duchess, who would have probably been less than welcome), her sister Princess Christian—both representing Queen Victoria—and Albert Victor of Wales, representing his parents, the Prince and Princess of Wales. The ceremony had to be slightly curtailed as the Kaiser's wife, Empress Augusta Victoria, was expecting another child, and according to the Empress Frederick there were also 'difficulties about rank and so on',[16] especially as the groom was regarded as being of less noble blood than his Hohenzollern bride. The *Tafel* (wedding breakfast), the *Fackeltanz* (traditional, very lengthy torchlight dance), the wedding ball, and other customary court functions were all omitted. However, there was a gala performance at the opera house on 17 November, at which Victoria wore her mother's wedding gift of a sapphire, diamond, and pearl diadem, with a large family dinner hosted by the Empress Frederick next day.

On the day itself, a private civil marriage ceremony at the palace of the Empress Frederick was followed by a religious service in the chapel of the Berlin Schloss. Victoria's cousin, Princess Marie Louise of Schleswig-Holstein, daughter of the Empress's sister Helena, thought that the service seemed exceptionally long and that everyone became very bored.[17] Another of the guests, Emily Loch, Helena's lady-in-waiting, included some photographs of the occasion in an album; she called the bride, 'a buxom young lady with a sweet unsmiling expression'. Emily Loch's biographer was undoubtedly not alone in speculating that thoughts of Alexander might have passed through Victoria's mind.[18] Even more to the point, Count Alfred von Waldersee, Chief of the German Imperial General Staff, noted in his diary on the day of the ceremony that he was quite sure the couple did not suit each other and he was convinced that the marriage could never be a happy one.[19] It had become, in effect, a match to appease the Kaiser more than anything else.

For others it was a day of great emotion. When the young couple turned from the altar at the conclusion of the service, the Empress clasped Victoria in her arms and whispered to Adolf, 'Be good to her.'[20]

Unhappily, for some of the family, the wedding was overshadowed by a petty quarrel which ignited into one of the fiercest arguments the family had seen for some time. As wife of the heir to the Greek throne, Sophie had decided that she ought to become a member of the Greek Orthodox Church, and she had intended to inform her brother Wilhelm, as head of the family. Wilhelm decided to delegate this disagreeable matter to his wife, thinking that Sophie was more likely to listen to another woman from the family than to him, and that she would think twice about arguing with someone who was eight-months pregnant. Before Sophie had a chance to speak to him on the subject, and shortly before her sister's wedding, she received a command from the German Empress, her sister-in-law Augusta Victoria, to come and see her at once. The Empress told her haughtily that as head of the Lutheran Church, the Kaiser would never permit her to change her religion. If she disobeyed him and did so, she would 'end up in hell'. Taking the perfectly understandable point of view that her loyalty was to husband and new country rather than her overbearing brother, Sophie politely but coldly told her sister-in-law that it did 'not concern anyone here' and she did not need to ask anyone. Her brother Wilhelm, she said, had 'absolutely no religion'; if he had, then he would never have behaved to their parents as he did. Whether she went to hell or not was her own affair, and it was not for the Empress to concern herself about it. The Empress reportedly grew purple in the face with rage, and became so excited that the doctors had to be called in to see her.[21]

The next day the Kaiser angrily called on his mother to deliver Sophie an ultimatum: if Sophie entered the Greek Church without his permission—which he certainly would not grant—he would forbid her to set foot in Germany again as long as she lived. He telegraphed to King George of Greece that should she persist, 'I shall no longer regard her as a member of my family and will never again receive her. I beg you, as far as in your power, to dissuade her from her intention.'[22] The King replied with great restraint that he did not feel justified in trying to influence his daughter-in-law. Though he was too tactful to do so, he would have been entitled to point out that she was not only married but also a Greek subject, and was thus no longer under the jurisdiction of her elder brother. King George, the Empress Frederick wrote to Sophie, 'has the best of the argument, and I admire him for being so gentle and moderate, in spite of such provocation.'[23] When the Empress Frederick declared that she was equally supportive of her daughter's intentions, and agreed that it was none of the Kaiser's business, Wilhelm complained that she had nothing but scorn and contempt for Christian belief. She told him that if he carried out his threat to ban Sophie from Prussia, she would no longer visit or receive him. He told one of his officials that his mother treated him so badly that he was reduced to tears.

Sophie had never been close to her brother, and was not at all worried by his outbursts. Like her sisters, she had been greatly irritated by her sister-in-law's airs and graces since becoming Empress, and though angered by this latest episode, perhaps it was little more than she expected. The Empress Frederick suggested she might like to try to hold out an olive branch by writing him a conciliatory letter, explaining fully her reasons for wishing to adopt the Greek faith. When he still would not give way, she sent her mother an open telegram saying: 'Received answer, keeps to what he said in Berlin, fixes it to three years. Mad. Never mind. Sophie.'[24]

When the German Empress gave birth to a son, Joachim, three weeks prematurely on 17 December, the Kaiser held his sister responsible as she caused his wife to become unduly excited. When the Empress Frederick came to call upon her daughter-in-law to enquire after her health and that of the new baby, the Kaiser would not allow her to enter the castle, and immediately gave orders that she was to be taken back to her carriage and sent away. Bitterly hurt, she wrote to Moretta, then on honeymoon with Adolf, that she and Sophie were both heartbroken at their parting and felt that she would never come back to Berlin. Only the fact that Mossy was still unmarried and needed her protection against the Kaiser as head of the family prevented her from making a complete break with him.

Queen Victoria longed to mediate in the matter and bring some common sense to bear on her grandson. She wrote to Queen Olga of Greece that as soon as she had heard of the arguments, she sent word to the Kaiser that she did not blame Sophie at all. It was her opinion that where another person's conscience was concerned, 'one must be tolerant and not condemn, as one has not the right to do so'.[25]

The baby Joachim was none the worse for having appeared too soon, but the Kaiser would not be pacified. The argument continued for several months, and as late as May 1891, the Kaiser was complaining almost hysterically to Queen Victoria. Sophie, he wrote to her, had caused 'an awful scene in which she behaved in a simply incredible manner like a naughty child that has been caught doing wrong'. The Empress became ill, gave birth prematurely, 'and for two days was at death's door'. He then had an interview with Sophie, in the presence of the Empress Frederick and Crown Prince Constantine, in which his errant sister entirely refused to acknowledge him as the head of her family or church, declared that she would not have anything more to do with the Hohenzollern family, or with their country, and refused to answer any questions he asked her about her conversion, declaring that it was nobody's business. '[If] my poor Baby dies,' he concluded on a note of hysteria, 'it is solely Sophie's fault and she has murdered it.'[26]

The Kaiser and his sister had never been close, and now they would never find themselves at ease in each other's company. While she was on a family visit to St Petersburg in the spring of 1892, Sophie was reported by Count Waldersee to have spoken bitterly about her brother and said, among other things, that the whole family thought he was mad.[27] As most of the Romanovs had scant admiration or respect for the Kaiser in the first place, it served as little more than confirmation of what many of them had already been inclined to believe.

The family quarrel did have one unexpected benefit: it brought their brother Heinrich back firmly onto the side of his mother and sisters. For some years he had been inclined to side with his brother and Charlotte and against his parents in family arguments, mainly as he was weak and easily swayed, faults which the then Crown Princess Friedrich Wilhelm readily recognised. But once he was betrothed to his cousin Irene of Hesse, whom he married in May 1888, he became more assertive. His displeasure at the family argument over Sophie's change of religion completed the process. From that time onwards, it was noticeable that he kept his distance from the Kaiser and Empress, and that he seemed correspondingly on much better terms with his mother and younger sisters.

The whole family was well aware of how obstinate Wilhelm could be, and Victoria spoke for them all when she told her mother in a letter that his entourage was too afraid of him to give him any advice.[28] Despite her contempt for her sister-in-law Empress Augusta Victoria, Princess Charlotte claimed she was equally angry at Sophie's decision to change her religion, while Victoria and Margaret were 'absolutely infuriated' by their brother's attitude. Victoria tried to take on the role of peacemaker between mother and son, telling the former that Wilhelm had 'a curious sort of character' and did not like to admit when he had been foolish. When she was shown copies of the angry correspondence between Wilhelm and Sophie, she remarked how sad it all was, but keen as ever to make excuses for him, she thought that perhaps his answer was misunderstood '& he may regret his hastiness [sic] & rough ways towards his little sister!'[29]

As the family had hoped, Kaiser's threat to banish his sister did not materialise. Queen Victoria wisely predicted that nothing would happen as long as Sophie continued to visit Germany as usual and Constantine was with her. When the family travelled to Heidelberg to visit the Empress Frederick in May 1891, the Crown Prince of Greece arrived a few days before his wife in order to see what reaction, if any, there would be from his brother-in-law. As he had suspected, there was none at all. The Kaiser was due to make a state visit to Britain, and did not wish to incur the wrath of his formidable grandmother. Count Leo von Caprivi, who had succeeded Bismarck as chancellor the previous year, interceded on Sophie's behalf, and the Kaiser allowed her to visit her mother. Afterwards the Empress Frederick wrote to thank him, not merely for giving permission for her to see Sophie, but for not placing any obstacles in their visit.

As a new member of the family, Adolf found it prudent to keep his distance from any unpleasantness between the siblings. When Victoria travelled to Bad Homburg to join her mother and two youngest sisters in June 1891 to mark the third anniversary of Kaiser Friedrich's death, Adolf did not accompany her; his excuse was that he could not to leave his squadron at such a time. The Empress Frederick was bitterly offended; she had invited him three times. This, she wrote to Queen Victoria, was the price she had to pay for Moretta having married a German prince who was only a captain in the cavalry, and who had to do everything that Wilhelm wished.[30] Only a few months earlier the Empress's eldest daughter Charlotte, who thrived on tittle-tattle, told officials at court that on her visit to Victoria and Adolf at Bonn, her mother attempted to stir up feelings against the Kaiser, telling her son-in-law 'dreadful stories about him'.[31] Aware that his marriage had depended on the Kaiser's favour, Adolf preferred not to be drawn into the disharmony.

In spite of Charlotte's gossiping, relations had been smoothed over, at least for the time being. In the summer of 1892, when Constantine and Sophie arrived in Copenhagen to stay with their Danish relations, Wilhelm sent word to his sister that he hoped her forthcoming visit to see their mother at Homburg would do her good.

Empress Augusta Victoria had made a name for herself by her inflexibility over issues concerning personal morality and religion; modern dance crazes and divorced men and women at court incurred her particular wrath. In this she was strongly supported, and to some extent influenced, by three long-serving ladies-in-waiting, known by the younger and less reverent members of the family as the 'Hallelujah aunts'. Even her husband found their excessive piety wearing on occasion. The independent-minded Victoria incurred the wrath of one of them in particular, Countess Teresa von Brockdorff, the Mistress of the Robes, at a court function on the Kaiser's birthday. She was standing with her back to the window, and as there was a particularly cold east wind on that January day, she slipped a sable boa over her shoulders to keep warm. Suddenly she felt a sharp tap on her back and a sharp whisper: 'Take that boa off.' Turning round angrily, she found herself face to face with the Countess, who told her that she could not possibly wear such a garment while her sister-in-law the Empress was not wearing one. Victoria glared at her and retorted in a whisper that the boa would remain on, and that she would speak to her brother about it afterwards. She kept her word, and that was the last time the matter was ever raised.[32]

As the one remaining unmarried child, Mossy had been her mother's constant companion since Victoria's marriage, and was destined to remain as such during the next few months. At around this time, mother and daughter were both caught up in a difficult situation which had been largely of the Kaiser's making. Having alienated Russia over his failure to renew the Reinsurance Treaty on its expiry in 1890, the Kaiser was faced with the likelihood of an alliance between two powerful hostile neighbours. He was thus anxious to improve Franco-German relations.

The Kaiser had never revised his unfavourable opinion of France as a nation. During the previous year he had refused to let his mother and sisters visit Queen Victoria while she was in Aix-les-Bains, on the grounds that he was duty-bound to uphold a law which had been passed by his grandfather in 1887, forbidding any prince or princess of the Prussian house to cross the French frontier without the Kaiser's consent. However, the Empress had long been a regular visitor to Paris, and as a patron of the arts her presence would be less likely to attract hostility than his. Her role, the Kaiser decided, would be to invite French artists to participate in an international art exhibition in Berlin. When the scheme was suggested by her old friend Count Münster, now German ambassador to France, she was so delighted to be of use that she did not realise her son was using her to pull chestnuts out of the fire.

Margaret accompanied her mother when she arrived at Paris on 19 February 1891 under the alias Countess Lingen. It was a venture which also appealed to the eighteen-year-old princess, who was an amateur artist herself. While the family were in Greece for the wedding of Sophie and Constantine, she had often been seen sketching in the open air. However, a small, vociferous right-wing group in Paris, eager to make political capital out of the Empress's presence to try to discredit Germany, was watching her progress very carefully. Versailles and St Cloud were scenes of happier days in 1855 when she, her brother, and parents had been guests of Emperor Napoleon and Empress Eugenie, but later of national humiliation and defeat for the French—the press claimed that she had gone out of her way to insult France, had refused to receive the Russian ambassador and his wife, had gone to see mostly Jewish art exhibitions in the city, and had bought nothing in the shops while she was there. The painters who had accepted invitations to exhibit in Berlin were accused of dishonouring their country, and when the German press replied in kind, feeling between both countries rose to such a pitch that the Empress and her daughter were advised to leave France at once.

Although mother and daughter enjoyed a close relationship, there were tensions, even if they remained below the surface. After her sisters were married, Margaret felt lonely, and missed the companionship of friends her own age. She also had yearnings for the gay party-loving society life of Berlin, something which her mother was keen for her to avoid, especially as she did not want her youngest daughter turning into another version of the frivolous, scandal-loving Charlotte. In addition, she had something of a complex about being ugly, because her nurse had instilled in her the belief that she was. Many years later, as a grandmother, she told one of her grandsons that she discovered her parents had ordered the nurse to tell her thus, in order to prevent her from becoming vain. It was evidently a resentment which she carried throughout her adult life.[33]

After a formal family visit to Buckeburg, Victoria and Adolf began their honeymoon tour which took them to Vienna, and also the Mediterranean. In Rome they were entertained by King Umberto and Queen Margherita, and in Cairo by the Khedive. Here Victoria had the strange experience of touring the Khedive's harem, accompanied by his chief wife. Like many other nineteenth-century tourists in Egypt, they sailed down the Nile, visiting Thebes and the Valley of the Kings, though Adolf was more interested in shooting and fishing than in inspecting ancient remains.

Finally, after a stormy sea voyage, they arrived at Piraeus in Greece where Sophie and Constantine were waiting to give them a hearty welcome. The Crown Princess had hoped that her sister and brother-in-law would be able to enjoy a few quiet weeks with the family, but her plans were altered. After staying there for only a few hours, the newly married couple returned hurriedly to Germany. Victoria had suffered an early miscarriage. Sadly, she would never conceive again. Perhaps significantly, like so many other unpleasant aspects of her life, this sadness was never alluded to in her memoirs. Yet she never ceased to long for children, and her inability to have any was a severe blow to her, especially every time another niece or nephew was born to her sisters.

On their return to Germany, Victoria and Adolf settled in the Schaumburg Palace at Bonn. The Prince was devoted to his regimental duties which often took him away from home, and Victoria was often lonely. To find some distraction, she threw herself into furnishing their home in her favourite English style. As the Empress had noted, Adolf was 'thoroughly German in his ways, so I fancy Vicky has a hard time of it to get things done nicely.'[34]

Left on her own, Victoria became increasingly unhappy. When her husband took up his military duties, she admitted, it was not to her liking. She disliked his absences on long army manoeuvres, and began to lose weight through excessive dieting. Her husband and mother were very alarmed when her doctor declared that she did not eat enough or lacked the right items in her diet. 'She still refrains from milk, sugar, butter, bread and sweets,'[35] wrote her anxious mother to Sophie. But the Empress and Adolf both recognised what the underlying problem was. Adolf was also longing to become a father, and made an effort to spend more time at home. He was affectionate, supportive, and tactful enough not to reproach her for not being able to conceive; nor did he give any indication that he recognised she had only married him in the hope of finding fulfilment through having a family. She was aware how he felt, and described him as 'one of the kindest, noblest and best of husbands imaginable, chivalrous, courageous and humane.'[36]

Their mutual disappointment was underlined by Sophie's ever-growing family. When she sent her mother a picture of her with baby George, the Empress wrote on Easter Sunday 1892, 'How poor Vicky and Adolf long for a baby, I see a shadow of sadness pass over their faces when they look at a photo of you and the baby.' In spite of that, the Empress assured her that they were 'very happy together and their little *ménage* is so harmonious and peaceful.'[37]

Victoria dutifully accompanied Adolf on his shooting and hunting expeditions. As she had a passion for tennis, he built her a court in the grounds of their home on which she, friends, and her household could indulge themselves to their heart's content. Every year they took regular holidays to Scheveningen in Holland for the sea bathing, and while they were there they would call on the former Queen Emma and her young daughter Queen Wilhelmina, who Victoria described as 'a good-looking, fresh-complexioned girl, rather reserved but with charming ways'.[38] There were also regular visits to her mother and sister Margaret, and less frequently to Greece to visit Sophie and her children.

Margaret, who was now her mother's constant companion, and had always been thought by the family to be closer to the Empress than her elder siblings, would not remain single for long. At twenty years of age, Mossy was a pleasant-looking if not strikingly attractive young woman. As far back as 1889 it was said that Crown Prince Ferdinand was interested in her as a possible bride.[39] By the spring of 1892 there was talk of her becoming betrothed to the Tsarevich. It was a curious echo of

Herbert Bismarck's scheme involving her sister Sophie a few years earlier, a plan which was said to have been vetoed by Tsar Alexander III because her father had died of cancer and she might bring contaminated blood into the Romanov family—an ironic theory in view of subsequent history. One wonders how differently events might have turned out if Margaret, who was destined to become the mother of six healthy sons, had become Empress of Russia. Some newspapers reported that she and the Tsarevich were about to become betrothed and that she had begun to prepare for entry into the Orthodox Church. Nevertheless, the Empress Frederick had a passionate dislike of the Romanovs, especially Tsar Alexander III, since his vendetta against Alexander of Battenberg. The ambassador Bernhard von Bülow thought such a match would be very unlikely, and that the Kaiser would never agree to it because it would turn the princess 'into a full-blooded Russian and enemy of Germany', and stir up no end of trouble for her brother.[40] A less controversial suggestion was a match with Christian, eldest son of Crown Prince Frederik of Denmark, the future King Christian X, but this likewise never came to anything.

The next matchmaking scheme to be put forward was for Margaret to become the bride of her British cousin Albert Victor, Duke of Clarence. In May 1890 Queen Victoria had told him that she thought there was no princess who would be more likely to suit him than this cousin in Germany, who was not exactly pretty but 'has a very pretty figure, is very amiable and half English with great love for England'. Mossy was invited to stay with the family at Sandringham in the spring of 1891, but the possibility of a match went no further. It was thought that Mossy was too German in outlook and personality for the liking of the Princess of Wales, who had nursed a powerful anti-German feeling since Bismarck had waged war against her father's country in 1864, taking the duchies of Schleswig and Holstein from Denmark. She did not want any sister of Kaiser Wilhelm as a wife for her son. Francis Knollys, the Prince of Wales's private secretary, told Sir Henry Ponsonby, who held the same post for Queen Victoria, that he personally thought Margaret would make an admirable choice; he suspected the Prince of Wales believed likewise, but not his wife, whatever her views on her niece's character. 'I wish the Princess would see these things differently,' he wrote, 'but she likes the girl herself and were it not for the objection I have mentioned, would I think rather like her for a daughter-in-law.'[41] Others thought that Mossy seemed more English than her sisters, particularly Sophie who prided herself on being thoroughly German, as some of her Greek in-laws would later discover.

Margaret was more attached to her mother than her sisters, and this, it was noted by a journalist, was affecting her decisions on taking a husband:

this affectionate devotion on the part of the young girl has interfered on at least two occasions with the arrangement of a brilliant matrimonial alliance projected for her, as she declared that it would be impossible for her to be happy so far away from her mother and from home as would have been her case had she accepted the proposals made.[42]

The princess who might have become the consort of two future kings, or even a future Tsar of Russia, was destined to find a husband in Germany instead. It was noticed that she had taken a particular liking to Max of Baden, a German cousin. However, in May 1892 Friedrich Karl, known as 'Fischy' in the family, a son of the Landgrave of Hesse, asked the Empress Frederick for her daughter's hand in marriage. She replied to him that up until then, Mossy had regarded him as a dear cousin and a brotherly friend; the request to propose came as a shock to them both:

[We had not realised] that your feelings had changed from being merely those of a friend and relation. It is a very great surprise and Mossy is in a state of tremendous excitement. She is so conscientious and devoted to duty that she must first consider the great change in her life, and she could only say yes if she felt she could return in full measure the feelings you have for her.[43]

At first Margaret was reluctant to give Friedrich Karl an answer, but after a few days her mind was made up, and when he proposed to her in June she said yes. Aged twenty-four, Friedrich Karl was the third son of Landgrave Friedrich of Hesse-Cassel, who had died in 1884. His eldest son Friedrich Wilhelm had succeeded him as Landgrave, but drowned in the Pacific four years later on a voyage from Batavia to Singapore. As he was unmarried, the title passed to his eldest surviving brother Alexander, who was blind and an invalid. It was therefore likely that Friedrich Karl would become the heir to the title and estates. He could already trace close kinship to the royal family. His mother Anna was a daughter of Karl of Prussia, the late younger brother of Kaiser Wilhelm I, while on his father's side he was a first cousin of the Princess of Wales, King George of Greece and Empress Maria Feodorovna, wife of Tsar Alexander III of Russia. He and Margaret were third cousins, both being great-great-grandchildren of King Friedrich Wilhelm III.

Although the Empress felt sad at the prospect of losing her last unmarried child, she thought it 'a great relief to have her decided'. She assured Queen Victoria of her great joy at the impending match. Fischy, she said, loved her daughter devotedly and was 'really a very nice boy, so steady and quiet though rather timid and delicate looking.' She described him as intelligent and cultivated with a taste for learning and art and writes charming poetry. I am so sorry that you do not know him. He is not rich and does not possess a place of his own, but he is quite comfortably off and I hope will be independent. You can imagine how upset and agitated I am, although very thankful to think my own precious darling will be happy—though I shall now be left quite alone.[44]

Queen Victoria's good wishes were tempered with mild disapproval. 'I hope and believe it is what you wish,' she wrote, 'but I think Mossy ought not to have left you so soon at any rate…. As Fischy has no place of his own, could they not chiefly live with you?'[45] However, the Empress lacked her mother's possessive streak; she knew how the marriage of her youngest sister Beatrice to Heinrich of Battenberg had been blighted by Queen Victoria's insistence that they live with her. Although she realised it would mean loneliness for her, the Empress refused to consider the suggestion that the young couple should live with her.

The engagement was met with approval all round, though the Kaiser was unenthusiastic. He gave his consent, but always keen to find fault, he remarked privately that his future brother-in-law was 'too thin and too solemn'. The Empress Augusta Victoria also received the news coldly, apparently put out—or so the Empress Frederick believed—because Margaret had not chosen Ernst Gunther, titular Duke of Schleswig-Holstein, the Empress's fun-loving bachelor brother and black sheep of the family. His sisters were generally ready to forgive him for his misdemeanours, but the Empress Frederick called him 'a most foolish young man', while her daughter Victoria dismissed him as 'that idiot', and even more pointedly, Count von Eulenburg, one of the Kaiser's closest confidantes at court, likened him to 'a rutting stag in spring'.[46]

Shortly after the engagement, the Empress Frederick asked Eulenburg whether the Kaiser would allow Friedrich Karl to leave the army once he was married. The Kaiser replied that this could not be done; his future brother-in-law had a 'philosophising, melancholy' character and needed more contact with soldiers and military service.[47]

This was not the only criticism the Kaiser made. To Queen Victoria, he said he thought it 'a poor match', and that he would never have given his agreement if his sister had not been a younger child and therefore of little importance. However, the Queen knew that Friedrich Karl's own opinion of future brother-in-law was not favourable; he was well aware of the Kaiser's callous behaviour in years past to his mother and sisters.[48] Aside from this, the Hesse-Cassel family had nursed a deep resentment of the Hohenzollerns since the annexation of Hesse at the end of the Six Weeks' War in 1866. Although Friedrich Karl had been born two years after this event, he had inherited the family grudge. Moreover, he was never at ease with the stiff atmosphere of military headquarters in Potsdam, or the attitude of Prussian officers of elite regiments with their perpetual drinking, gambling, and duelling.[49] Nevertheless, he was astute enough to realise that, unlike his eldest brother-in-law, his bride-to-be and her mother did not conform to the Prussian Hohenzollern stereotype.

The wedding was originally scheduled for 20 November, but in the autumn it was postponed until early in the new year. According to *The Graphic*, the festivities would 'be conducted with pomp, Kaiser Wilhelm being determined to pay especial honour to his last unmarried sister'.[50] Among the guests who arrived in Berlin were Heinrich and Irene, Victoria and Adolf, Prince Albrecht, Regent of Brunswick, the Duke and Duchess of Connaught, Prince and Princess Christian and their elder daughter Princess Victoria Helena, the Dukes of Cambridge and Edinburgh, King Albert of Saxony, and the Tsarevich. Those who had hoped to be there but were unable to come included the Prince and Princess of Wales, and the Crown Prince and Princess of Greece, as Sophie was expecting another child and was not well enough to travel. The King and Queen of Denmark had also planned to attend, but it proved to be an exceptionally cold January, and the shipping routes between Denmark and Germany were made hazardous by ice. Another potential guest had been Ernst, Duke of Saxe-Coburg Gotha, whom the Kaiser had announced his intention of inviting. The Empress Frederick's elderly uncle had disgraced himself in her eyes, not only by his immoral behaviour and flagrant infidelity, but also by his denigration of the memory of Kaiser Friedrich to curry favour with the new Kaiser and Bismarck. She had declared that if Duke Ernst was coming to the wedding, then she would not attend. Although it was unlikely that she would have absented herself from the ceremony of her beloved youngest daughter, particularly as it was taking place in Germany, this threat was sufficient to make the Kaiser think again, and therefore no invitation was sent to the ageing roué at Coburg.

The national and local newspapers in both countries were filled with details of the forthcoming programme of ceremonies and the bride's presents. A ball was held on 20 January in the White Hall, followed by a family banquet two days later, a state banquet the next day in the White Hall, and the Empress Frederick's state banquet the day after that. The wedding was to be on 25 January, the thirty-fifth anniversary of the Empress's own wedding. The civil marriage was to be held in the hall at her Berlin palace, Unter den Linden, performed by Herr von Wedel, the minister of the household, and then the bride and her mother would drive in state to the Schloss at Berlin for the church ceremony. The young couple would then leave for Neue Palais.

The Empress's presents to her daughter included a set of diamonds and emeralds consisting of a diadem, necklace, earrings, brooch, and bracelets. There were also 'several very fine dresses', including one which had been a present to the Empress from Kaiser Wilhelm I, who had received about a hundred sable furs from the St Petersburg Merchants of the First Guild on his visit to Russia in 1873. Queen Victoria's presents comprised a quantity of Honiton lace, Indian shawls, and a silver tea service, while the Kaiser gave her a diamond necklace, and the Prince and Princess of Wales sent two diamond bracelets. King Umberto of Italy presented Margaret with a diadem, necklace, brooch, and earrings of diamonds set in gold and adorned with large black pearls, and two bracelets of diamonds and rubies, which he had given to her mother in trust when he and Queen Margherita came to Germany for their goddaughter's christening in 1872.

On the morning of the wedding itself, 25 January, proceedings began with the family all having breakfast together. In the words of the Empress Frederick, reporting to the absent Sophie, 'arrangements, telegrams, etc., took up the short time until our hurried luncheon'. It was then time for the bride to be dressed; her mother wrote that she was 'serious and grave but [shed] no tears' throughout the morning. In the afternoon the civil marriage contract was signed at a ceremony in the long dining room, with crowds of guests looking on. Then the bride and her mother drove away in a gala coach drawn by six horses, 'getting in and out of the carriage being very difficult with the bridesmaids carrying Mossy's train'. They arrived at the Berlin Schloss and proceeded up the great staircase, 'with a noise of trumpets and drums enough to stun you'. As they walked to the chapel, 'she held herself so well and bore herself with such natural dignity and grace that everyone was charmed with her.'[51]

According to one reporter at the scene, the ceremony was 'of a most imposing character', although the chapel 'in itself formed a poor setting', being 'a bare inartistic structure in the worst style of the Italian renaissance, with round arches.' The floor, he continued, 'was indifferently clad with scraps of tawdry carpet. The whole had a singularly cold and depressing effect.' Describing the service itself, the reporter observed:

> the music stilled the Court chaplain; Dr Dryander stepped forward from the altar, attended by the clergy of the Court, all wearing the customary Lutheran black, with white bands, throwing the colour of the pageant into relief, and delivered a fifteen minutes' harangue on the nature of love. He struck, unfortunately, a false key, and it appeared to be a subject in which he was not too well versed, the sentiment being that of Wolfram von Eschenbach in *Tannhauser*, whereas the characteristic of the whole scene was grandly Pagan. Moreover he wanted a little fire and

life. Dr Dryander might also have considered the Princess, who had now been kneeling for thirty five minutes, evidently in discomfort. At last he brought his nuptial discourse to an end, and the bridal pair were brought to the front, and exchanged rings....[52]

After the benediction had been given, the Kaiser and Empress came forward to kiss the bride and bridegroom. The choir struck up Handel's *Erschallt Trompeten Heher und Lant*, the procession reformed, and the ceremony was over. Commenting on the wedding in a letter to Sophie two days later, the Empress Frederick thought that the groom looked 'very pale and grave' as they stood before the altar. She approved of the music, but noted, '[I do not] like the weddings here as you know, I think them stately but stiff and mournful. Nothing but ceremony! Nothing joyous!' She also found it 'exhausting' and from eight in the morning until midnight she did not have a chance to sit down except at meals.[53] Emily Loch, who was there in attendance on Princess Christian, also noted that they 'stood from more or less 4.30 till 10.15'. She also considered that the bride 'did it all beautifully and looked very nice', although the groom 'looked very ill',[54] probably meaning ill at ease in the presence of such company rather than unwell.

In order to compensate for the snow outside and bitterly cold weather, all the rooms had been heated as much as possible for the comfort of guests. The job had been done so effectively that at a reception held by the Kaiser and Empress, at least one or two people fainted from the excessive temperature. Among them was the Tsarevich, who had been presented with the Order of the Black Eagle, which required him to wear a particularly uncomfortable red cloak throughout: 'I nearly died of heat in it,' he later said.[55] Matters were also not improved by the behaviour of Ernst Gunther, who was always more than ready to be an entertaining host to the guests, far more so than his imperial brother-in-law. During the wedding celebrations he treated the Tsarevich to a bachelor's evening of Roman punch and dancing girls, causing them both to miss a dinner laid on partly in honour of the Russian heir on 27 January, Kaiser Wilhelm's birthday. The Kaiser was furious, and overlooking the fact that one of his closest relations by marriage had been responsible, despatched a priggish letter to the Tsar complaining of his son's behaviour, his 'proclivities for vice', and his 'disregard for the decencies of life'.[56]

4

'One hated oneself for not being able to relieve her' 1893–1901

For Victoria and Adolf, the desire for their own family was still as strong as ever. Although she enjoyed leading an invigorating outdoor life, Victoria's health sometimes gave cause for concern. About two years after her wedding she had to undergo treatment at a clinic in Bad Schwalbach for various conditions including persistent anaemia, backache, unexplained loss of weight, and stomach cramps. It is thought that she might have suffered from porphyria, the hereditary illness which blighted the life of her eldest sister Charlotte and Charlotte's only child Feodora.[1]

Added to Victoria's continued frustration at her inability to bear a child was her sorrow at the news of the death of Alexander, former Prince of Bulgaria, on 23 October 1893. Broken in health and spirit, he died at thirty-six of peritonitis, leaving his widow with two small children, the second a baby only three weeks old. 'Happy as she is with Adolf,' the Empress wrote, 'the death of the one she first hoped to marry cannot but make a deep impression on her.'[2]

At around this time the diary of Victoria's eldest sister Charlotte, containing scurrilous gossip about the family and important figures at court, accidentally found its way into circulation. It disappeared in 1892, when she and her husband Bernhard were on holiday in Greece and Palestine with their close friend Count Leberecht von Kotze, an official at court, and his wife. Society life in Berlin was notorious for its scurrilous gossip, and Charlotte was at the centre of much of it. The diary dealt a mortal blow to her relations with the Kaiser, with whom she had generally got on well in the past. Among the comments were references to 'poor Vicky', described as being 'many-sided' because of the affairs she had enjoyed before and possibly during her marriage.

During the same period, anonymous letters, written in a disguised hand in block capitals and posted in Berlin, were also in circulation. They began being sent after a party hosted by Charlotte and Ernst Gunther in January 1891, and were addressed to and from members of the family and Berlin society. With obscene comments and snobbery, they targeted members of the court who were not from the highest ranks of the aristocracy.

There seems to be no solid evidence of infidelity on Victoria's part, and entries from the diary of a woman who was notorious for her love of lurid, spurious gossip can hardly be accepted as reliable fact. Nevertheless, there were allegations of flirtations and a possible affair between Victoria and Baron Hugo von Reischach, a Lieutenant of the Garde-du-Corps and husband of one of the princesses of Hohenlohe, who subsequently became gentleman-in-waiting to the widowed Empress Frederick. This liaison 'formed the theme of quite a number of the anonymous letters, in which the princess was charged with every kind of indelicacy, while the unfortunate baron was ridiculed in connection with the modernity of his nobility'. Various other love affairs of 'poor Vicky' prior to her marriage were likewise discussed in a blunt manner. She was said to have been so infatuated with Count Tivadar Andrassy, elder son of the famous Austro-Hungarian statesman, that in order to escape her attentions, he was forced to resign his position at the Austro-Hungarian Embassy in Berlin and leave the Prussian Court. 'If it is like this now,' said one of the letters, 'what in Heaven's name will it be when "Vicky" marries!'[3]

Although some of this undoubtedly related to the period before she was married, the insinuation was that Victoria also had affairs with other men behind Adolf's back later on. Several hundred such letters were sent over a period of four years, and most were, not surprisingly, destroyed by their angry recipients on arrival. About thirty of them survived, and they were later placed in the hands of a military tribunal. In June 1894 Kotze was arrested on the Kaiser's orders and charged with authorship of the letters, but released after his innocence was established beyond doubt. He felt compelled to defend his honour publicly by challenging those of his accusers who had not apologised to a duel. The first of his accusers to take up the challenge was Baron von Reischach, who succeeded in wounding Kotze by shooting him in the thigh. Another accuser, Baron von Schrader, also came forward. He lost the duel and died of his injuries the following day. The affair soon passed into history, but from many quarters there was strong criticism of the Kaiser for permitting such contests to take place between his officials.

After the scandal broke, one can only assume that Victoria was more forgiving towards her eldest sister than the Kaiser was. He and the Empress, whose brother and brother's French mistress were strongly suspected to have been responsible for the letters, were both furious with Charlotte. She and her husband Bernhard were henceforth banished from Berlin, with the latter posted to the sleepy provincial town of Breslau, away from the centre of society life and where Charlotte could do no harm.

A few months after her husband's death, the Empress Frederick had bought Villa Reiss, a property near Kronberg, which had previously belonged to a tea merchant. She had never felt comfortable living in Berlin, and after thirty years she was pleased to find a place she could call her own. Fortuitously, at around the same time she was left a legacy by her friend Maria, Duchesse de Galliera, which enabled her to purchase an additional 250 acres of adjoining land and plan the building of a magnificent new house. It was on the suggestion of the newly married Princess Victoria that they should call it Friedrichshof in memory of Kaiser Friedrich, and over the front door were carved the words 'Frederici Memoriae'. The Empress employed the Ernst Eberhard von Ihne, official architect to Kaiser Friedrich and now to his successor, to supervise the building, and sent him to England to study country house architecture. The result was a house built partly in German Renaissance style.

In the spring of 1894, Friedrichshof was completed and ready for the Empress to move in. At last she had a home where she could arrange her collections of paintings, curios, books, and all the other items she had collected over nearly half a century, and entertain her guests and family as she wished. Among the first family guests to visit was Kaiser Wilhelm. Although she did not particularly relish him inviting himself and his suite so soon after the house had become habitable, she could hardly refuse to receive her eldest son. Inevitably, visits from her daughters were to be much more welcome. In May she entertained Sophie, who came to call on her; she left her two small sons, George and Alexander, to stay with their grandmother while she visited Denmark. The Empress welcomed Sophie back on her way from Scandinavia, and was almost inconsolable for a while after they had departed.

After their wedding, Margaret and Friedrich Karl made their own home at Schloss Rumpenheim, the eighteenth-century family house near Frankfurt. They were not long in starting their own family, and by April her mother and grandmother were aware of a new arrival on the way. 'Poor thing, I pity her so much,' Queen Victoria wrote. 'It is really too dreadful to have the first year of one's married life and happiness spoilt by discomfort and misery.'[4] The Empress made plans to be with her daughter for the confinement shortly before Christmas, but was forestalled when Margaret gave birth to a son on 24 November, a month early. Writing to Sophie, the Empress noted that his arrival had taken everyone by surprise, and 'of course he found nothing in order for him'.[5] He was named Friedrich

Wilhelm, in memory of the grandfather whom he had never known.

Eleven months later, on 20 October 1894, Margaret gave birth to a second son. Once again it was a premature arrival, frustrating the plans of the maternal grandmother who had hoped to be at Rumpenheim in time for the confinement. A telegram that her daughter had been taken ill was despatched at 4 a.m., followed by another under three hours later to say that the child had arrived. The Empress ordered her carriage immediately and reached her daughter about three hours later. Mossy and Fischy, she reported to Queen Victoria, were delighted that it was another 'nice healthy boy', weighing over 7 lbs.[6] He was given the name Maximilian.

Two years later, when Margaret was expecting again, the Empress arrived on time. She visited her daughter and son-in-law at Rumpenheim and was thrilled at the birth of twin sons on 6 November 1896. They were named Philipp and Wolfgang. At the time, their father was confined to bed with rheumatic fever, and for a fortnight after the birth, the Empress was kept busy carrying notes between husband and wife, as they were not allowed to see each other for fear of infection.

The Empress Frederick was an indulgent grandmother. Although she could be quite intellectually demanding, and liked to be able to share her cultural enthusiasms with the family, she enjoyed allowing the youngsters to run around and make as much noise as they liked. Some members of the household were irritated by the sight and sound of the Hesse-Cassel boys racing around the corridors at Friedrichshof, as they shouted at each other and blew their toy trumpets. To the end of her days, the boys' cousin Victoria Louise, only daughter of Kaiser Wilhelm, resented what she thought was preferential treatment shown by her grandmother to her young Hesse-Cassel and Greek cousins when they came to stay. Whenever Victoria Louise and her brothers went to the house, their visits were preceded by warnings from their tutors and governesses to be on their best behaviour. However, they came less frequently than the other grandchildren of the Empress, who always regretted that she was allowed to see them so little. Empress Augusta Victoria had never been at ease with her mother-in-law, and tensions still lingered between the Kaiser and his mother; they were reluctant to allow her to see too much of their sons and daughter.

In March 1895, the childless Prince Waldemar of Lippe-Detmold died suddenly. His brother and successor Alexander had been declared insane, and Victoria's husband Adolf was named in Waldemar's will as Alexander's regent. He gratefully accepted the position, recognising that the responsibilities and duties involved would undoubtedly give some much-needed focus to their lives. He also hoped that their new social demands might help distract Victoria from brooding on her childlessness.

Victoria loved Detmold, with its fifteenth-century Schloss and the surrounding woods and hills of the Teutoburger Wald, and she threw herself into the new role with enthusiasm. Husband and wife took part in a programme of joint visits to almost every town and village in the principality, and were pleased by the enthusiasm with which they were received. For the first time in her life, she had real duties and responsibilities. Her days were full as she supported Adolf in his work and she conscientiously filled the traditional role of Landesmutter, trying to improve the land and the conditions of the people.

However, the Count of Lippe-Biesterfield, the head of a junior branch of the family, registered a legal challenge to the late Prince's will. He was supported by the Landtag of Lippe, but the body's decision to have the succession dispute settled by a court in Leipzig was contested by several of the German federal princes, to whom it appeared to be a curtailment in principle of their sovereignty. They demanded that the matter should be decided by a compromise between the parties involved. They accordingly agreed to accept the decision of an arbitration tribunal presided over by Albert, King of Saxony; as the Empress Frederick noted, the German princes 'were getting up agitation in the Detmold press and Landtag'.[7] Although the Kaiser proved supportive of his brother-in-law and sister, and the Landtag voted to accept the regency of Adolf, the uncertainty was a constant worry. It was one of the rare occasions in which the siblings were completely united. Charlotte also defended the claim of her younger sister and brother-in-law, asserting that a decision in favour of the Biesterfeld line would be 'a victory for democracy'. The mother of the reigning Countess, they said, was a former shop assistant, and her father had been an American smallholder. The 'Biests', as they called the family, were 'disgusting, common' people who had taken on princely airs, and the German princes could not be expected to tolerate 'such a pack of worthless wretches'. What, they asked, would their father or grandfather have said?[8]

In the autumn of 1895, Victoria and Adolf paid a short visit to the Empress, but for some reason—most probably boredom on the part of Adolf—they curtailed their stay. Queen Victoria was indignant when she heard about it from her daughter she was 'so provoked,' she wrote, '[at Moretta] hurrying off before the time (far too short as that was) that she agreed to stay'. If any of her sons-in-law had dared to behave that way, she said, she would have been furious. A daughter had her duties to her widowed mother who had no child living with her, and she thought their early departure showed extreme selfishness on the part of Adolf.[9]

In Athens, Sophie was busy beginning to learn Greek. Within four or five years of her wedding, she could inform her mother with pride that she could speak the language of her adopted country to the new ministers who came to palace receptions. In August 1893 she gave birth to a second son, whom she and Constantine named Alexander. The occasion was marked by salutes from Russian and British warships at the port of Piraeus.

Even as an adult, Sophie was just as fond of England as she had been as a child, and she always enjoyed visiting her mother's country. In particular she adored visiting department stores in London, and found it a useful way of passing the time; she was supervising the building and furnishing of a more comfortable home in Athens for the family, as well as an English-style cottage in the grounds of Tatoi. After one shopping session at Maple and then Liberty, Sophie wrote enthusiastically to her mother that she had 'screamed at the things to Tino's horror, but they were too lovely! No, those shops, I go mad in them! I would be ruined if I lived here longer!— Divine shops!'[10] Victoria and Margaret could count themselves fortunate that, like their eldest sister Charlotte, they had made comparatively modest marriages and remained within the borders of Germany. A few months after the birth of her first daughter, Helen, in May 1896, Sophie was to find that being the only one of her siblings to marry into another royal family and settle in a foreign country brought its own problems. At the time the island of Crete was under the rule of the Ottoman Empire, but many Greeks wanted to reunite Crete with the mainland.

In January 1897, Sophie wrote to her mother—who copied the details in a letter to Queen Victoria—that she was extremely keen to attend her grandmother's diamond jubilee celebrations in London that summer if it was possible:

> …but there will be many things to prevent it, also, I fear, fighting in Macedonia and Crete; there is no possibility or hope of preventing people here, they are _poussés à bout_, exasperated; they make their preparations secretly, they <u>do not</u> speak about it in public! It will be known soon enough!! This is, alas, the result of the Powers doing nothing decisive enough and letting matters drift.[11]

Queen Victoria and Lord Salisbury, her prime minister, took note of the warnings. The following month Salisbury wrote to her that he thought if the Cretans were allowed to unite with Greece, the Macedonians would rise against the Turks, thus leading to a fierce struggle between Moslems and Christians throughout the Ottoman Empire. If Britain was to support the Cretan insurgents at this time, it would risk a quarrel with the other Great Powers; his correspondence with their ambassadors had just confirmed that they were unanimous in their intention that Crete should remain part of the Ottoman Empire. While he realised it was impossible not to feel sympathy for King George of Greece, it would be 'easier for him to give way to the Great Powers than to put himself at the head of all the revolutionary forces' in the area, which he would soon find too violent and unruly to keep under control.[12]

During the next few weeks, Sophie continued to confide in her mother, who again copied the details in a letter to Queen Victoria, of her 'fright and horror of the future', and how it 'makes one mad to think of all the misery that may yet come'. She firmly maintained that 'Even if the Powers do not give us Crete, they must know that never never will the Cretans rest, or the Island have peace, until they are Greek.'[13] She hoped that her eldest brother might offer them some support, but to her astonishment and anger, Kaiser Wilhelm sided firmly with the Turks. He showed himself to be unashamedly anti-Greek, and while she was prepared to accept— albeit reluctantly—that national and political considerations might take precedence over family obligations between brother and sister, she was furious at the tone of his utterances. To him, the King of Greece was 'a worthless and ill-mannered man', and his sons were 'louts without any education'.[14] The Empress Frederick asked Salisbury to convey to him her disgust at his behaviour, professing herself 'astonished and shocked at his violent language against the country where his sister lives. He could surely have abstained from such language.'[15] It distressed her that she was unable to do anything for Sophie but offer her sympathy.

Greece declared war on Turkey in April 1897. Had King George not done so, declared Sophie's cousin, another George, Duke of York, the King ran the risk of being assassinated by his angry subjects, who were spoiling for victory on the battlefield. Constantine was appointed Commander-in-Chief of the grossly unprepared Greek army, and it was on him that much of the blame if not the responsibility for the country's ultimate defeat would fall. Kaiser Wilhelm continued to make clear his antipathy towards Greece and his indifference to the plight of her royal family, with government newspapers in Germany urging the extinction of country, people, dynasty, and all. Sophie felt bitterly at her brother's attitude, and the Empress pitied her greatly: 'pray do not think I suffer less because I am William's mother.'[16]

Within less than a month, the Greek forces were driven back. Sophie begged her brother in Berlin to help prevent further bloodshed by hastening the mediation which had been proposed by the Great Powers. He insisted to her that he could not do anything until Greece recognised the autonomy of Crete and withdrew her troops from the island. Only after this had been done did the German ambassadors in Athens and Constantinople agree to enter into peace negotiations.

The vengeful Greeks, who had urged war in the first place, turned on their King and Crown Prince, accusing them of treason. Edward Egerton, the British minister in Athens, reported that crowds were gathering in Athens, intending to attack and storm the royal palace. One Sunday the customary prayer for the royal family could not be said by the metropolitan bishop because of the cries and hisses of the congregation. The newspapers were equally insulting and lacking in any sympathy. The Empress Frederick was particularly concerned about her daughter, and above all feared for her safety as well as that of her husband, children, and parents-in-law. 'Is it wise for you all to remain in the town?' she asked. 'Would you not be safer where there is no mob? Have you ever thought of having your valuables and jewels and papers packed up and sent on board a German or English ship?'[176]

Hostilities came to an end on 17 May, but it made no difference to the unpopularity of the royal family. Whenever they appeared in public, Sophie and Constantine were jeered at and spat on in the streets, and there were demands that he should be court-martialled. During the war, Sophie had found a positive role as she threw herself into the work of the newly founded Union of Greek Women, which involved itself in taking care of refugees, buying new medical supplies, fitting out hospitals, and giving lectures to volunteers on how to care for the wounded. Queen Olga had also been an active patron in the nursing field for many years, and Sophie followed her example, bringing over English nurses to help train the Greek ones. It proved a thankless task and nationalism inevitably reared its head, with Greek nurses taking exception to being shown a better way to do their work by 'foreigners'.

In addition to working long hours in Athens as she helped to nurse the wounded, Sophie visited Larissa, where she supervised hospitals for the wounded and dying. One of her achievements was to convert a large building which had recently been completed and intended as a military school into a hospital. When she was not making her rounds tending to the sick and injured, she and Queen Olga sat in on examinations of the Red Cross Nurses.

Meanwhile, Greece had to sue for peace, which was signed between both sides in September, and part of the price of defeat was being forced to cede minor border areas and pay heavy reparations. It was a national humiliation, and the popularity of the royal family fell accordingly, with calls in the army for major reforms and the dismissal of Crown Prince Constantine and the other princes from their command posts in the forces. Sophie was particularly distressed, and the Empress Frederick was very anxious, especially when it was rumoured that the Crown Prince might have to leave Greece for a while until the clamour had subsided.

Margaret and Friedrich Karl had already paid one of their regular visits to England in 1897, when they spent three weeks in April staying at Buckingham Palace with the Queen, and at Bagshot as guests of the Duke and Duchess of Connaught. Two months later they returned to England, leaving Kronberg on 18 June, accompanying the Empress Frederick for the celebration of Queen Victoria's Diamond Jubilee. As it was intended primarily as an imperial commemoration, other heads of state were not invited; Kaiser Wilhelm eventually agreed to stay away, complaining that as the Queen's eldest grandchild he felt he had every right to be there. However, other family guests were welcomed; Charlotte, Bernhard, Victoria, and Adolf were among those who visited London later that week. Charlotte, Victoria, and Margaret all rode in the same carriage in the procession from Buckingham Palace to St Paul's Cathedral for the service of Thanksgiving on 22 June. The following evening they attended a state performance at the opera, Covent Garden, to see and hear selections from *Tannhauser*, *Romeo et Juliette* and *Les Huguenots*, and the evening after that they were among guests at a dinner party at Buckingham Palace. On 29 June they saw a performance of Gilbert & Sullivan's *Yeomen of the Guard* at the Savoy Theatre. The days passed all too quickly, and on 3 July they left Windsor and returned to Germany.

For Victoria and Adolf, the few days they spent in England were overshadowed by bad news. Despite the Kaiser's fury at not being asked to adjudicate in what he called the 'wretched Lippe affair', the King of Saxony had accepted the invitation to preside over the court which was convened to study the case. The Kaiser had unequivocally taken the family's side, but on this occasion they were in the minority. In his memoirs some thirty years later, Bernhard von Bülow, Imperial Secretary of State for Foreign Affairs at the time, commented scathingly on his master's attitude to the controversy. He noted that 'by dint of continual and violent intervention, with particularly little tact,' the Kaiser 'managed to give offence not only to the German princes, who stood with few exceptions on the side of Biesterfeld, as the one supported by legitimate titles,' but to the rest of the German people. Barely ten years after his 'harsh and violent opposition' to his sister's intentions to wed the former Prince of Bulgaria, he aimed to show his mother and sister that 'if he stretched forth his Imperial right arm to protect them, he would impose his will'.[18] For once his will did not prevail, and the succession of the principality was awarded to the Lippe-Biesterfelds. There was to be no happy homecoming for Victoria and Adolf; they returned to Detmold at once where Adolf formally offered his resignation as regent to the Landtag. As the Empress wrote to Sophie, it was a severe blow to them both: 'That charming home, lovely country and fine houses, position, occupation, future all gone! Poor Vicky is most unlucky in life, if only she had had children, she would not mind so much.'[19] They went back to Bonn, and although they were moved by the affectionate send-off given them by the people, it was scant compensation for yet another disappointment.

Adolf took up his regimental duties once again, while Victoria returned to the usual round of tennis parties and visits to relations. In 1898 they accompanied the Empress on a visit to Queen Victoria at Balmoral. Marie Mallet, one of the Queen's maids of honour, noted in her diary that they seemed to be 'a devoted couple,' and that Victoria had 'changed much and for the better in her personal appearance, being now a graceful good-looking woman instead of a particularly plain girl.'[20] Like many others, she failed to notice the sadness beneath the smile. While her mother had had to put up with years of frustration, disappointment, and eventual misfortune—though not as a result of an unhappy marriage—Victoria had obviously learned much from her maternal example in making the best of a difficult situation.

For Sophie, the end of the war had not meant an end to her hard work. For several months she continued to toil in the hospitals, comforting the wounded and encouraging the overworked nurses and doctors in places such as the English hospital in Chalcis, which had been singled out for its efficiency and good practice. When Empress Eugenie, the widow of Napoleon, Emperor of the French, visited Athens in August 1897, she was most impressed by Sophie's work and reported as much to Queen Victoria, who had long been a close friend. The Queen passed on her comments to the Empress Frederick, who had been in Athens and seen Olga and Sophie, who she said, 'did not <u>look</u> ill and who she [Olga] spoke of in the highest terms, her anxiety, her devotion. You would have been pleased to hear her.'[21]

Both royal ladies, Queen Victoria observed, had also been nursing wounded Turks. The Queen thought it was only fitting that Sophie and her mother-in-law should be accorded some special recognition for their services, and asked her private secretary, Sir Arthur Bigge, whether it would be feasible. Bigge had to inform her that national considerations precluded a royal Order of the Red Cross being presented to either, unless the Crown Princess was to receive it as a British princess, which was not really possible. The Queen then asked if it would be possible to alter the statutes of the order so that the sovereign could bestow it on any royal person irrespective of nationality. Nobody could raise any valid objections to this, and in December 1897, Queen Olga and Crown Princess Sophie were both awarded the Royal Order of the Red Cross. By this time, the Empress Frederick had told William Boyd Carpenter, Bishop of Ripon, that it had been a 'most trying and harassing' year, especially as 'the anxiety and sorrows about poor Greece were terrible'.[22]

Fears of assassination among the Greek royal family would soon come close to realisation. Dismayed by the general mood among his people after the war, King George seriously considered abdication. In February 1898, he and his daughter Marie were riding in Athens in an open carriage, when two gunmen opened fire on them. They were unhurt, but the coachman and one of the horses were wounded. At this, the general hostility to the royals was reversed almost overnight. Nevertheless, the family's recent unpopularity had shaken the Crown Princess badly, and she would never forget just how volatile the Greeks could be. Later that year at Athens she met Maurice de Bunsen, then first secretary at the British Embassy in Constantinople. He recorded afterwards that he had found her very agreeable, 'and we had a long *tête à tête*. Life at Athens is evidently a great trial to her.'[23]

In September 1898, the Empress Frederick had a severe fall while out on her horse, and was never really well again. Shortly afterwards, cancer of the spine was diagnosed, but only her closest friends and most trusted members of the family were told at first. She impressed on them the importance of keeping it secret, as she did not wish the German public to know. Even before learning the real cause of her mother's trouble, Margaret suspected that it might be something more serious, and she spent as much time nursing her at Friedrichshof as her family duties would permit. Victoria and Sophie also took turns at their mother's bedside, but as they lived further away it was less easy for them, particularly for Sophie. She was the only one of the Empress's six children who was unable to be with her for her sixtieth birthday, by which time she was 'in torment' for several hours of the day. Margaret took on the job of writing her mother's diary and letters for her, especially when the sick woman found the pain too severe to hold a pencil and had to resort to dictation.

Several members of the family, including the Empress's children and all of her children-in-law, except for Bernhard, and her nephews Ernst, Grand Duke of Hesse and Albert of Schleswig-Holstein, visited her at Friedrichshof for luncheon on 24 May 1900, Queen Victoria's eighty-first birthday. Family photographs were taken on the terrace outside to mark the occasion. It was fitting that a celebration for the matriarch from whom they were all descended should have been what turned out to be the last major family gathering of her lifetime.

Victoria, Adolf, Margaret, Friedrich Karl, and their four sons all spent Christmas 1900 at Friedrichshof. It was a particularly sad festive season for them all, as the princesses knew that neither their mother nor their grandmother would live much longer. The Queen was steadily becoming frailer. She was greatly concerned by British military reverses in the Boer War, and aggrieved by the recent losses of her second son Alfred, Duke of Saxe-Coburg Gotha in July, and a much-beloved grandson, Christian Victor of Schleswig-Holstein in October. It was a mournful echo of the situation thirteen years earlier when it was feared that the two sisters' gravely ill father might predecease his own parent, the nonagenarian Kaiser. However, the Empress clung on to life, despite being bedridden and in agony much of the time. Queen Victoria and her household had gone to Osborne House for Christmas, but early in the new year she took to her bed for the last time. Her family gathered around her as it became evident that the increasingly enfeebled matriarch, weakened by a series of strokes, was sinking. Once or twice she rallied slightly, but everyone knew that the end could not be far off. She passed away on the evening of 22 January 1901, aged eighty-one.

To Margaret fell the painful duty of breaking the unhappy, if hardly unexpected, news to her grief-stricken mother. The Empress had been virtually bedridden for some weeks, and was no longer well enough to travel, let alone go to England for the funeral. Her second and fourth daughters and their husbands represented her as they travelled to England and took their places with other members of the family and foreign royal dignitaries for the obsequies at Windsor on 2 February. Always eager to be the centre of attention, the Kaiser was already there, having left Berlin in mid-January on the advice that the Queen was dying. He went to Osborne House where he helped support her on her deathbed with his one good arm. As the Empress Frederick had remarked dryly when she was told, 'Willy will bury Grandma while she is still alive.'[24] After the final ceremonies, Victoria and Adolf returned to stay with the Empress at Friedrichshof.

A constant stream of visitors, mostly members of her family, came to visit the dying Empress. The most important was King Edward VII, who arrived in February on what was his first journey abroad after succeeding his mother on the throne. Among his entourage was his private secretary Sir Frederick Ponsonby, to whom the Empress entrusted her letters to her mother, which she did not wish her eldest son to seize and destroy, and which he would edit and publish as *Letters of the Empress Frederick* some twenty-seven years later, after a certain amount of soul-searching. During their time in Germany, Ponsonby also had the opportunity to enjoy a few leisurely walks around the gardens with his hostess's daughters. He had known Victoria as a girl, and he 'found her full of go, but unhappily married'. He was not alone in having seen some signs of stress or marital disharmony which others, but not everyone, had either missed or were too discreet to comment upon. Sophie and Margaret, he considered, 'were charming and most anxious to help and make the meeting [between King and Emperor] a success.'[25]

Ponsonby found that family dinners every evening were hardly lively affairs, although the Kaiser kept small-talk going. Sophie and Margaret would cut in tactfully 'if the conversation seemed to get into dangerous channels and one always felt there was electricity in the air when the Emperor and King Edward talked'. One night the superstitious King was alarmed when he realised that thirteen people had sat down to dinner, but on reflection he told Ponsonby that it did not matter as Princess Friedrich Karl was *enceinte*. In fact, events would prove that they had been safer than he realised at the time, for his niece Margaret was carrying not one child but two. Three months later, on 14 May, she gave birth to a second set of twin boys, who were given the names Christoph and Richard.

During these months the Empress Frederick's secretary, Count Götz von Seckendorff, considered that the sufferings of his mistress were only exacerbated by the many children, relations, and retinues coming to the house; he described the latter as having become half hotel, half hospital.[26] Victoria seemed to agree with him, and she was as keen as he to try to keep some sense of order. Her eldest sister Charlotte was also present at times, but proved a less regular visitor. Not everybody appreciated Victoria's vigilance; in particular Marie Mallet, one of those who was only allowed to see the Empress from a distance, noted, 'she is feared and detested here. The poor little court is torn by petty intrigues and at this terrible solemn moment.'[27] Perhaps she failed to appreciate that the princess was racked by a sense of guilt at such a stressful occasion lasting several months. Her heart torn by the sight of her mother's agonies, Victoria admitted in her memoirs that 'one hated oneself for not being able to relieve her'.[28]

Although she was expecting a fourth child at the end of the year, Sophie also came to Friedrichshof to undertake her share in the vigil. In one of her last letters, the Empress encouraged Sophie, before she left Athens, not to lose heart: 'countries and states are not made in a day, and long and many are the struggles they have to go through.'[29]

By the last days of July the end was evidently near, and relatives were summoned to their mother's side. On 4 August the newspapers announced that the sixty-year-old Empress was sinking. Early in the evening of 5 August, Victoria, who had spent much of the time at her mother's side in her bedroom on the first floor, went out into the garden for fresh air. A servant came to call her back to her bedside when the end was very near, but she was too late to be present when she breathed her last.

'Trying to repress her feelings' 1901–14

Though it had been a merciful release from suffering for her, the Empress Frederick's three youngest daughters were particularly devastated by their mother's death. Victoria was the one who perhaps felt their loss the most, being without any children of her own and in what was evidently a less than satisfactory marriage. 'She had been my dearest friend,' she later wrote, 'and all through my life I had looked up to her as possessing most wonderful qualities of mind and heart. Her loss has left a blank in my life which nothing and nobody else can ever fill.'[1] To an old governess who had written the family a letter of condolence, Sophie replied that while they were thankful she had peace and rest at last, 'the blank she leaves behind is too terrible & you know what we have lost in her; it seems all like a dream, not possible to be true!'[2]

In her will, the Empress had appointed Margaret her literary executor, and she left Friedrichshof and most of its contents, including her jewellery and art collection, to her. Among these possessions were Queen Victoria's letters to the Empress, a total of 3,777, covering the years from 1858 to 1900. Although it was unusual for a husband in Germany to live in his wife's home, Margaret was committed to maintaining her mother's house, which entailed considerable expense; she and her family moved in and made it their primary residence. Kaiser Wilhelm asked Margaret whether she would also take their mother's place as Chief of the 80th Fusilier Regiment. It was perhaps a magnanimous decision on his part, especially as he considered that as his mother's eldest child, she should perhaps have bequeathed her home or at least her most precious possessions to him. Nevertheless, he already had several private as well as state residences in Germany, and with regard to her collections, he was always more of a dilettante rather than a true devotee of fine arts. As a second son, Friedrich Karl had never had a primary claim on his family's ancestral home.

Moreover, his mother-in-law had recognised and approved of his cultural interests. She knew that he would appreciate her decision to allow him such a generous share of her estate, even though it would be an expensive house to maintain.

There had been another reason for the Empress's bequest. During the war between Prussia and Austria in 1866, Hesse had been one of the small independent German states which had taken the side of Austria. After the overwhelming Prussian victory, Hesse-Cassel was annexed, and the reigning dynasty into which Margaret had married was deposed and their fortune was confiscated. These events had made the then Crown Princess of Prussia and many members of her own family uncomfortable. Leaving her youngest daughter Friedrichshof in her will was some way, she believed, of righting a wrong from so many years ago.

It was with some reluctance that Friedrich Karl moved into the house, for the newly built castle was less to his taste than his old home at Rumpenheim. Though he was devoted to his wife and their six sons, he was by nature a solitary character who had always enjoyed writing poetry and collecting books, and the transition to family life was not always easy for him. It was also quite likely that he found the constant presence of his mother-in-law a little overpowering. The young Princess Friedrich Wilhelm of Prussia had found her mother's maternal influence difficult to escape from in her early days as a married woman, and history evidently repeated itself. Although less possessive than her own mother, the widowed Empress probably found it more difficult to let go of her youngest daughter, and this almost certainly created problems for the newly married Prince and Princess Friedrich Karl of Hesse-Cassel. Nevertheless, what had not initially been the most harmonious of marriages improved with time after the Empress's death as they adapted to their new life in a new home.

Although Margaret loved to play the piano and was an enthusiastic amateur artist, she was never quite as dedicated to the latter hobby as her mother had been. Like her sisters, she had not fully shared in their mother's joy of collecting items for their own sake, and all three of them may sometimes have felt that they lived more in a museum than a home. More an outdoor person by nature, Margaret had a passion for animals, especially horses. For her, the ideal day at home generally began with a ride early in the morning, then returning to play the piano until the rest of the family and household were awake.

Victoria and Sophie had also been devoted to their mother, but their enthusiasm for the great parental house near Kronberg was not completely boundless. Three years before the Empress's death, Crown Princess Marie of Roumania described her cousin Sophie after a stay in Friedrichshof: 'I found her very nice, she is intensely bored there.'[3]

Though the death of the Empress Frederick succeeded in drawing her eldest son and her three younger daughters together, united in their sadness, it could only be temporary. There were outward displays of family unity for the sake of form, such as the presence of all four princesses and their husbands at Berlin to celebrate the Kaiser's forty-third birthday in January 1902—an occasion to which their cousin George, Prince of Wales, was also invited. Yet they did little to mask the differences that lay beneath the surface.

Although there was little love lost between them, Margaret was still keen to try to do what she could to keep relations as amicable as possible between her brother and their uncle, King Edward. Uncle and nephew, so very dissimilar in character, had never liked or felt at ease with one another, and the differences between them became more marked with the passing years. Even so, tentative efforts were made by governments and family on both sides to try to bring them and their representatives together. In August 1905 Margaret and Friedrich Karl invited the Kaiser and Sir Frank Lascelles, British ambassador in Berlin, to lunch at Friedrichshof. The meal went pleasantly enough, but as an effort of diplomacy it could hardly succeed where government initiatives had failed.

During the previous month, Paul Metternich, the German ambassador in London, reported to Prince Bernhard von Bülow, the imperial chancellor, on a conversation he had had with the Crown Prince and Princess of Greece and Prince and Princess Friedrich Karl of Hesse-Cassel, who were staying together at Seaford, on the Sussex coast, and at Buckingham Palace. At lunch one day, the Crown Princess told him how alarmed she was at the anti-German sentiments she had found at the British court. It was a source of great sadness to her, as England and Germany, she believed, were destined to co-operate together. King Edward, she stressed, also wanted the best of relations between both countries, despite 'his momentary annoyance', which she ascribed 'to his jealousy of his Imperial nephew's greater talents'. A meeting between them, she was convinced, 'would certainly do much to blow away the clouds on both sides'. Admiring her brother as she did, and having strong pro-English feelings, Margaret deeply regretted 'the irritability displayed here [in England]', agreeing with Metternich that there was no reason for it, 'as we had done nothing against the English'. Princess Friedrich Karl reiterated her sister's comments, and 'confirmed the existence of an anti-German spirit which verged on foolishness'.[4]

There were regular social exchanges between the royal and imperial family members on both sides of the North Sea. In August 1906 King Edward came to take the waters at Marienbad, as he did on a regular basis. On this occasion his itinerary included a brief visit to Homburg, Kronberg, and Friedrichshof, where he had lunch and dinner with the Kaiser, Margaret and Friedrich Karl, and the Crown Prince and Princess of Greece who were staying there at the time. It was a perfectly amicable rendezvous, but of no great importance; journalists tried to look for any major consequences of the meeting, but without success. As *The Times* reported a couple of days afterwards, more responsible sections of the German press 'have now abandoned the attempt to draw unwarranted political conclusions' from the meeting between both sovereigns, while other journals 'refuse to be so readily convinced and continue to attribute to the informal intercourse between the two Monarchs a character which it does not possess.'[5]

Like her mother, Margaret was a great lover of England, and she and Friedrich Karl made a point of employing English nannies for their children. She had also become a close friend of Hilda Chichester, a lady-in-waiting to Princess Beatrice from 1912 until the latter's death thirty-two years later, and the two would keep in touch regularly over the next four decades. The Hesse-Cassel family and household struck acquaintances as being very English, and remarkably free from the ostentation of the average Prussian officer's family which was so prevalent in other homes, particularly in that of the Kaiser. English was generally spoken in the family, and remained the princes' first language, even as adults. Throughout his life, Christoph usually wrote to his mother in English, while Philipp, who was in England for a while every year before the First World War, and his wife Mafalda, daughter of King Victor Emmanuel of Italy, whom he married in 1925, would nearly always speak English to each other. Some years later Sir Henry 'Chips' Channon, a British Member of Parliament, noted in his diary that he had spent an agreeable morning with Philipp of Hesse, and that they talked among other things of how so many European royals had a cockney accent acquired from English nannies.[6]

The Hesse-Cassel boys were less military-minded than their Hohenzollern cousins. While they were all staying together in Berlin during the winter of 1902, they looked at a painting of a cavalry squadron in gleaming uniforms, while shells exploded above their heads. The Kaiser's daughter Victoria Louise, who was aged twelve at the time, explained proudly that her father had commissioned it, and had given detailed instructions to the artist. Young Max of Hesse-Cassel told her that their father had told them war was not like that at all. He said that it was not nearly so clean and bright, and that shells tore the men and horses to pieces. If anybody dared to paint war pictures, showing battles as they really were, it would be too discouraging for the soldiers. His male cousins immediately rounded on him and tried to impress on him how wrong he was.[7]

Philipp and Wolfgang were sent to be educated in England, at Bexhill-on-Sea. When they started in September 1910, Margaret took the opportunity to combine the occasion with one of her regular visits to relations. On her return to Germany she wrote to Miss Chichester of 'a delightful week in beloved England', noting that the school 'really seemed excellent in every way'.[8] During another visit around this time, they all attended a birthday party for the spinster Princess Victoria, second daughter of King Edward VII. Although she was in her thirties at the time, the entertainment included various novelties and diversions with small children in mind, including fireworks that released parachutes containing Japanese ivory carvings for the youngsters to collect. At one of these gatherings, Philipp was so engrossed in collecting up the items afterwards that he did not notice his parents had left. In a panic he went up to King Edward, the only person he recognised, grabbed hold of his legs, and said tearfully that he was lost. Not knowing who the lad was, the King asked him who was his mother. 'Mossy,' Philipp replied. The King roared with laughter as he called a page, and entrusted him with the duty of returning the boy to his family.[9]

By the time of her mother's death, Sophie was the mother of three children and expecting a fourth. After the birth of her first two sons, a daughter Helen followed in May 1896, and the third son, Paul, in December 1901. All three of the sons would succeed their father as King at various times during the turbulent history of the Greek monarchy. In February 1904, they were joined by a second daughter, Irene.

Although it was not an opinion held by everyone who knew the family, according to the memoirs of an anonymous courtier, published in 1929, Sophie was said to be the most English of the children. Not only did she talk English to her husband and her own children, but the courtier said he often heard her speaking English frequently at Friedrichshof, apparently without any trace of a foreign accent.[10]

Sophie and Constantine enjoyed a happy domestic life on the whole, even if it was not quite the perfect example of marital fidelity that the marriage of her own parents, or that of her maternal grandparents, had been. Like his own father, Constantine had something of an eye for the ladies, and was not beyond taking the occasional mistress. The best-known of these was Paola von Ostheim, a woman who helped in the military hospitals during the wars, described by Nona Kerr, a lady-in-waiting, as 'a most unattractive female'. When a very concerned Sophie asked King George what she could do about it, King George shrugged and told her that she should ask Queen Olga for advice. In other words, what could not be cured must be endured. Miss Kerr, who disliked Sophie and thought she left much to be desired as a wife, considered that her personal shortcomings had been responsible for her husband seeking companionship and other comforts: 'the Crown Princess has only herself to thank for all this as she had made [her husband's] life unbearable for some years.'[11]

Like Margaret, Sophie was determined that her children should have an English education. While she learned to speak Greek perfectly, with her children the first language was always English. Every summer her two younger sons, Alexander and Paul, and her two elder daughters, Helen and Irene, were educated in England. She herself spent part of every summer at Eastbourne, generally taking her children with her and spending some of her time at Windsor with her cousins, and the rest of the time at the Grand Hotel on the south coast.

Yet life in Athens was rarely tranquil for the family. After the disastrous Greco-Turkish War in 1897, the Military League, a collection of army officers, threatened to take over the government. King George told Sir Francis Elliot, the British ambassador in Athens, that he had no intention of being the puppet of a military junta, and it was rumoured that he was threatening to abdicate. By 1909 Elliot was reporting to the Foreign Office in London of the parlous state of affairs, and the navy was ordered to be on standby in case they were needed to rescue members of the Greek royal family.

Sophie and Constantine were compelled to leave Greece temporarily in September 1909; she wrote despairingly, '[there is] no longer any place for us in this country'.[12] They went to stay with Margaret and Friedrich Karl at Friedrichshof. At length the situation in Greece was resolved the following year. King George had insisted that he would not compromise his position as a constitutional monarch; faced with stalemate as well as no change in attitude from the Great Powers, Eleutherios Venizelos, the man who had called for the union of Crete with Greece and had therefore sparked the Greco-Turkish War, was appointed chief minister. The Military League dissolved itself, and the Crown Prince was reinstated as commander of the army. Yet when he and Sophie left Margaret in Germany to return home, Margaret wrote to Hilda Chichester that Sophie had found the parting 'harder than I can say'. Sophie and Tino would be going back to Athens 'to what uncertainty & unsettled state of affairs…It was too sad to see her trying to fight down her feelings'.[13]

When they were home, Sophie found the situation no easier at Athens than she had before. Elliot criticised her in a report to the Foreign Office of February 1911, commenting on her apparently 'irreconcilable attitude towards the party of reform, whom she identifies with the leaders of the military movement of 1909, which she cannot forgive.' Neither she nor her brother the Kaiser, he went on, 'realise the necessity for the reigning dynasty here of passing the sponge over the distasteful events of that year.'[14] Exactly a year later, he had not revised his opinion of her. He reported to the Foreign Office that in his opinion the Crown Prince had shown 'signs of realising the necessities of his situation and of allowing bygones to be bygones; but the Crown Princess maintains an uncompromising attitude, which is unfortunately encouraged by the German Minister and his wife.'[15]

From this, Sophie inadvertently acquired a reputation for being pro-German. It was something which would do the position of her husband and herself no good at all in the years ahead, yet nothing could be further from the truth. She had never forgotten how supportive Kaiser Wilhelm had been of Turkey during the war of 1897, a war which had dealt such a blow to Greek prestige.

Later, Elliot managed to find some words of praise for the Crown Prince and his wife in a subsequent report to the Foreign Office. In February 1913 he acknowledged that the Crown Prince had won the confidence and affection of his men, that the Queen had been indefatigable in the organisation of hospitals and refugee relief, and that the Crown Princess had 'directed her activities among similar lines'.[16]

By this time, the defeat of 1897 had been avenged. In 1911, Italy had gone to war with Turkey over the possession of Tripoli, and a year later the Balkan League comprising Serbia, Bulgaria, Montenegro, and Greece, launched a joint offensive against the Ottoman Empire. This time, thanks to the Crown Prince's hard work, the Greek army was far better prepared, and within two months he and his troops had won a major victory when the Turks surrendered the city of Salonika. The royal family's stock rose accordingly.

As in the previous conflict, Queen Olga and her daughter-in-law had been working hard at nursing wounded soldiers and organising field hospitals. This time they had a helper from the younger generation of the royal family—Alice, wife of the Crown Prince's younger brother Andrew. However, her zeal did not go down well when she chose to take some of the nurses which Sophie had directed to certain hospitals and send them elsewhere without consulting her. When Alice was asked to take charge of hospitals at Epirus during the final stages of the conflict, the Crown Prince was so exasperated by what he perceived as her meddling that he entrusted another sister-in-law, Marie, with the task instead. The entire staff of another hospital were left in no doubt as to his feelings on the matter when he exclaimed angrily, 'Why the devil is Alice coming here to mix up everything as she did in Saloniki?'[17]

There was evidently some antipathy between both women. In December 1912, Alice's husband reported to Nona Kerr that there had been 'a row with the Crown Princess', and that 'she had been beastly to Alice & then had gone for him.... I think she is really a bit mad'.[18] Princess Louis of

Battenberg, Alice's mother, maintained that Sophie was jealous of Alice's popularity and tended to indulge 'in the true German "Empfindlichkeit" (sensitivity), a defect which really is at times worse than a vice'.[19]

For the childless Victoria, the years between her mother's death and the First World War were uneventful, with little to break the monotony of her life. She had never been close to her brother the Kaiser, and though Bonn was often quiet, even dull, she had no desire to live in Berlin. While she made regular appearances at important family and state events, they provided little enjoyment for her, and she was happier leading a quiet life at Schaumburg Palace with Adolf, lavishing affection on her dogs and horses, perhaps as a substitute for the sons and daughters she was never able to have.

In February 1909 King Edward VII and Queen Alexandra paid a long overdue state visit to the Kaiser and Empress at Berlin. Victoria was undoubtedly pleased to see her British uncle again, but he had been suffering badly from bronchitis and the programme of events was disrupted at least once by his ill-health. She probably sensed that this would be the last time she ever saw him. Moreover it gave her no pleasure to spend time at her brother's court or indeed in his capital. When she met Daisy, Princess of Pless, at a court ball, she admitted that she hated Berlin. For her, it had become an unpleasant if not 'an impossible town to live in,' where she found that everything seemed 'very stiff and false'.[20]

Margaret and Friedrich Karl always felt at home in England; they enjoyed a particularly cordial relationship with their cousins there, and went to stay with members of the family almost every year. In May 1910 they were grief-stricken by the death of King Edward VII, the man who might have become Margaret's father-in-law as well as her uncle. 'I wish for nothing more than to go to dear old England again this year,' Margaret wrote to Miss Chichester in June, 'although it will be very sad, but how delightful it would be to see you all again. One can still hardly realize the King's death, it all came too suddenly.'[21] However, there was compensation a year later, when they were among the royal guests from Europe who were invited to attend the coronation of King George V and Queen Mary in June 1911. Among others who had arrived in London for what would be one of the final great pre-war gatherings were Margaret's sister Charlotte and her husband Bernhard, the German Crown Prince and Princess, Karl, Archduke of Austria-Hungary, destined to be the last Habsburg Emperor, and representatives from the reigning houses of Russia, Bulgaria, and Montenegro. Whether they were in Germany or England, they remained keen observers of the political situation in the country across the sea. That winter, Margaret looked with alarm on one particular government appointment at Westminster—that of a minister whom she regarded as a threat to Anglo-German relations. She considered that it really was 'terrible to think of Winston Churchill being First Lord of the Admiralty'.[22]

There was a moment of drama on one occasion in August the following year, when *The Times* reported that a dressing case belonging to Princess Friedrich Karl of Hesse had been stolen from her luggage at Victoria Station. It was a green leather bag embossed with a gold crown and her monogram, containing a Bible which had been a gift from her father with his signature on the fly-leaf, a diary, a travelling clock, several keys, a few letters, and a grey motor veil. The first item was of particular sentimental value, and the German Embassy was offering a reward for the safe return of everything.

A few days later a man who was described as 'the manager of a boxing establishment' appeared at Westminster Police Court, charged with feloniously receiving the bag. The valet and maid, who would have been able to testify as witnesses to having deposited the bag with the railway company, would not return to England to attend the court hearing. Margaret wanted to send sworn depositions as a substitute for their attendance in court, but the police could not proceed on this basis and the case was therefore withdrawn.[23] Whether the missing case and contents were recovered and returned to their owner was not recorded. Nevertheless, it did not deter Margaret and her family from paying further visits to England during the last years of peace.

By the beginning of 1913, after the Greeks had avenged their earlier defeat at the hands of Turkish forces, the royal family were more popular than they had been for many years. Now aged sixty-seven, King George was approaching the fiftieth anniversary of his acceptance of the crown, and he told his sons that he was planning to abdicate as he felt his life's work was done, and that he had earned the right to enjoy a more peaceful old age.

On 18 March, Sophie, who was seven months pregnant, was resting quietly on a sofa when a Marshal of the Court came to speak to her on a matter of great urgency. From the distressed look on his face, at first she feared that something must have happened to her husband, until he told her that His Majesty had met with a serious injury. Instinctively she realised that her father-in-law was dead. He had been shot while walking along the streets of Salonika by a Macedonian lunatic who was apprehended and committed suicide while in prison awaiting trial.

Accompanied by her eldest daughter Helen, Sophie went at once to the palace to comfort Queen Olga, who wept quietly, saying that it was the will of God. Constantine was now King of Greece, and at the age of forty-two, Sophie was Queen. Although they had come to the throne under tragic circumstances, in a way it had been at the right time, with their popularity at its height; Constantine had redeemed himself as Commander in Chief of the military forces, and Sophie was well regarded as a tireless worker on behalf of the war wounded. Once again, the prophecies made at the time of their wedding—that a new Greater Greece would come about once more under the reign of Constantine and Sophie—were remembered and talked about.

Margaret was particularly anxious that the circumstances of her sister's accession might affect her adversely during the later stages of her pregnancy (at the age of forty-two), especially as Sophie had generally had difficult confinements. Nevertheless, she was reassured that in spite of the King's assassination, which was, they all hoped, an isolated incident of terror, the general state of Greece seemed better and more stable. 'Greece was in a terrible shock, just at a time when my sister ought to keep calm,' she noted in April 1913. 'I cannot help feeling frightfully worried as she has been at death's door with every baby.' However, the expectant mother proved to be more resilient than might have been feared. 'Thank God she has kept well till now, & is frightfully busy, taking everything into hand,' wrote Margaret. 'I also think that in many a way the country may become more prosperous, & her life more satisfactory.'[24] On 4 May Queen Sophie gave birth to a third daughter, named Katherine. Queen Olga, King George V of Britain, his mother Queen Alexandra, Kaiser Wilhelm, and all the officers of the Greek army and navy were invited to be her godparents.

Shortly after ascending to the throne, King Constantine and Queen Sophie moved into the new palace at Athens, built beyond the grounds of the old one. Sophie had taken a particular interest in arboriculture and the environment, and she made it one of her missions in life to help with the reforestation of Greece. One scheme in which she became actively involved was the organising of nurseries from which young trees could be taken and planted in the countryside where needed, especially on the bare hills surrounding Athens. She and Constantine shared a keen interest in gardening during their spare time, and they converted the kitchen garden beside the palace into a model English country house garden with large lawns, cypress avenues, pergolas, ponds, and herbaceous borders. She also continued to devote herself to social welfare, actively cultivating her interest in hospitals, soup kitchens, district nursing, schools for domestic training, and kindergarten education. She started the Society for the Prevention of Cruelty to Animals in Greece, and was its first founder.

Throughout her life, Sophie, very much her mother's daughter, was passionately pro-English, in sympathies if not necessarily in personality. Ever since the quarrel about her change of religion, her relations with Kaiser Wilhelm had always been very strained. Yet because of her German birth, the Greeks and indeed most other European countries assumed that her sympathies always lay with Germany as a nation. Brother and sister only met on one occasion when Sophie was Queen. In 1913, on the last of his annual visits to Corfu, where he had purchased Achilleion, the late Empress Elisabeth of Austria's summer palace, the Kaiser invited Queen Sophie and Venizelos to dinner one evening. Aware of the ill-feeling between them, he deliberately seated them next to each other. Although Sophie kept her feelings to herself and was cordial enough during the meal, she was so angry that after they had finished, she requested a car and returned to Athens at once without formally taking leave of the Kaiser.

In March 1913, the Kaiser's daughter Victoria Louise was betrothed to Ernst Augustus, Duke of Cumberland and heir to the duchy of Brunswick. It was a particularly welcome marriage alliance, as it helped put to an end the last lingering resentment between the Hohenzollerns and the descendants of King George V, last King of Hanover, who had been deprived of his kingdom in 1866 when it was absorbed into Prussia after the Austro-Prussian war. Margaret considered her niece's engagement 'a great joy to us all, it was her great wish, & she fell in love with this boy at first sight'. The prince was 'particularly nice, & belongs to a charming family, & this is certainly the best solution to the long disagreement between both houses.'[25] Margaret and Friedrich Karl were among a large number of royals throughout the continent who were present in Berlin at the wedding on 24 May, a date deliberately chosen as it had been the birthday of Queen Victoria. The palace was so full that several members of the family, including Margaret, her brother Heinrich, her sister Charlotte and their spouses, had to be accommodated at the Hotel Kaiserhof nearby.[26]

After it was over, Margaret reported on the festivities to her friend Miss Chichester:

> [They] were a great success & all went beautifully but I thought them rather exhausting, a sign that old age is beginning to tell on me. The King & Queen [George V and Mary] seemed to be enjoying themselves & the public really gave them a splendid reception, so that for the moment all seemed so friendly, if only it could remain so.[27]

Though Kaiser Wilhelm and King George of Britain enjoyed a far more amicable relationship than the former ever had with King Edward, Margaret was not alone in regarding apprehensively the tensions between both empires; like many of the family, she hoped that amicable personal relations between crowned heads would translate into a wider détente.

It was unlikely that any of the guests realised that few of them would ever see each other again, and that it was the last time that the Kaiser and Empress, King George V and Tsar Nicholas would ever meet; it was to be the last great royal gathering of imperial Europe. Queen Sophie, who was still in Athens recovering from the birth of Katherine, and Victoria, who was ill with pneumonia, were both unable to attend.

Never the shrewdest member of her family, Victoria was very isolated from political life in Germany, and at the beginning of the century felt quite disengaged from the development of European affairs. Although she was shocked by news of the murder of Archduke Franz Ferdinand and his wife Sophie on their visit to Sarajevo on 28 June 1914, its implications passed her by. At the beginning of July, she left for a few weeks' holiday in Nordeney and only realised how serious the situation was when war was declared in the first week of August.

Meanwhile, in July Queen Sophie was staying in England and met Margaret and her sons at Victoria Station; they went to Eastbourne together where Sophie was staying. The following week, they visited Queen Alexandra at Marlborough House, and two weeks later, on 27 July, they called upon King George V and Queen Mary. By the end of the month, Queen Alexandra, who had never liked the German Kaiser, told them that she feared war was coming. Sophie and Margaret were so alarmed that they immediately contacted Karl Lichnowsky, the German ambassador in London. He reassured them that, in his view, there was no danger of war between England and Germany. Even so, they felt it would be best to err on the side of caution, and Margaret, Friedrich Karl, and their sons returned home on one of the last ships to leave Britain during those few remaining days of peace. Their son Wolfgang thought that, while the two countries would never draw swords, there were alarming signs throughout Europe. Large groups of soldiers were at all the railway stations, with considerable amounts of luggage, and there was an unsettlingly tense atmosphere everywhere.[28]

Within less than a week, on 4 August, Great Britain declared war on Germany. The days of happy royal family visits by the Hohenzollern princesses to their cousins in England were now consigned to history.

6

'Too cruel & too senseless'
1914–18

Although he was no lover of war for its own sake, and had made his feelings on the matter clear to his sons, Friedrich Karl believed that he had to serve his country to the best of his ability. He and his sons duly took up arms in the name of the Fatherland. Although he was offered a staff position, he rejected it and was appointed to command of the 81st Infantry Regiment, which he led into battle in the Belgian area of the Ardennes mountains. On 22 August, two days after they had crossed the Belgian border near Bertix, Friedrich Karl's regiment met a French contingent and suffered heavy losses in the resulting battle. In another battle on 7 September near the village of Etrépy, he was injured by grenade fragments that covered the left side of his body. From the shrapnel, and from pieces of his uniform, he contracted blood poisoning. He was admitted to hospital in Frankfurt, but an operation was only partially successful in removing the fragments. Repeated operations did not complete the process, and because of his injuries as well as a heart condition, he was pronounced no longer fit for combat.

Friedrich Karl's two eldest sons would be less fortunate. Maximilian, who according to his younger brother Wolfgang had always been their mother's favourite, had gone to the front with the Prussian 1st Life Hussars. On 12 October 1914, he was shot and seriously wounded by machine-gun fire in an engagement with British cavalry while fighting with his regiment at St Jean-Chappel near Bailleul, Flanders. He was evacuated by his comrades to a Trappist monastery at Mont des Cats, where the monks looked after him. When the British forces advanced and took control of the cloister, he was sent to a British field hospital, but his wounds were too severe and nothing could be done for him. As he lay dying, he told the British doctor who was attending him that he was a great-grandson of Queen Victoria, and he asked him to return a chain and locket containing his mother's picture to her. The doctor was killed a day or two later when a German shell hit the field hospital, but he had written a note to go with the locket, and it was sent to his widow in England. She passed it on to Queen Mary of England, who returned it to the bereaved mother at Friedrichshof, via Margaret, Crown Princess of Sweden and the Dowager Grand Duchess of Baden, both of whom were working for the Red Cross. As a senior royal family member in a neutral country, Margaret of Sweden, known in the family as 'Daisy', was able to act as a go-between for messages between her cousins and relations on opposing sides. Because of Maximilian's close relationship to the Kaiser, his body was carried to Caestre, a French town, and buried in secret.

The family were stricken with grief, and it was three months after the loss that the bereaved mother put pen to paper on the subject whilst writing to thank Lady Corkran, as Hilda Chichester had become on her marriage in 1913:

> Words cannot express what I feel like, nor how great my misery is. That boy was so much to me, & nothing will ever make the wound heal. Everything is unchanged here & very peaceful & yet so different. One often longs to wake up from this agonizing dream, for one sometimes cannot believe it is all true.[1]

Although Britain and Germany were now supposed to be the bitterest of foes, Margaret took some consolation in her continued friendship with Lady Corkran. Shortly after Christmas 1915, she told her what a comfort it was 'that things cannot change between us, dear Hilda, altho' the world has been turned upside down, & one often wonders how it is possible that all should have come as it has.'[2]

Another abiding sorrow was to befall the family within less than a year when the eldest son Friedrich Wilhelm, who was their father's favourite, met a similar fate to his brother. On 12 September 1916, while serving with the army at Kara Orman, Roumania, he was killed in combat. Another brother, Wolfgang, was serving with the same regiment, and asked to view the body; he noted that 'Fri' had had his throat slit by an enemy bayonet.[3] The thought that he had perished in this way made the news harder to bear. When they were told of his death, several members of the family gathered together at Kronberg and held a vigil throughout the night in his memory. Out of sympathy for his doubly bereaved youngest sister, shortly after Friedrich Wilhelm's death, the Kaiser ordered that Philipp and Wolfgang should be kept out of harm's way. The loss of a third son in the conflict would be almost too much to bear. Wolfgang was transferred to the staff of Field Marshal August von Mackensen, while Philipp was kept away from the front line entirely.

Once again, Margaret wrote to Lady Corkran of her desolation at this second bereavement:

Your kind sympathy in my overwhelming grief touched me very much
& I thank you with all my heart for two kind letters wh[ich] prove to
me once more what a kind friend you are ... you know how fond I was
of my two eldest, & will understand what I feel like, now that both have
gone. I can still hardly realize the terrible fact, only that the pain gets
worse & worse as time goes on.[4]

Frederich Wilhelm's body was brought home and buried in the chapel at
Friedrichshof. A different fate awaited the body of Maximilian. When the
villagers of Caestre learned that a nephew of the Kaiser had been killed
in battle nearby, they concealed his body and vowed they would keep it
a secret until all of the German forces had withdrawn from their country
and reparations were paid in full. Messages were sent from the German
side asking for the location of his grave, and the local priest replied that
he would only let the Kaiser know the prince's resting place once these
conditions were met. In 1920 Wolfgang appealed to the British authorities,
and his body was returned. The chapel at Friedrichshof was adorned with
banners bearing the family arms and became a place of pilgrimage. For
many years, after she had attended Sunday morning service, Margaret
went to pray in the chapel beside where her sons lay, and any guests who
were staying with the family at the time would do likewise.

Though she and Adolf had no sons to lose, Victoria also suffered as the
Fatherland was plunged into war. All of the imperial family had to deal
with the reality of blood relations fighting on opposite sides, something
which had bedevilled the British and German royal cousins and in-laws
ever since the Prusso-Danish war of 1864. Victoria was shocked by the
bitterness of personal feelings against German royals, especially herself,
the Kaiser's sister. Yet whenever she visited hospitals, it did not stop her
from making a point of talking to German and British wounded soldiers
alike, treating them as equals. She was perhaps too naive to appreciate the
changes which accompanied the war.

As a professional soldier, Adolf was attached to the Eighth Army Corps,
and within a few days of the outbreak of war he had to leave for army
duties. Victoria established a small nursing home which enabled her to
make her own contribution to the work of the German Red Cross.
Husband and wife were apart from each other on the date of their silver
wedding anniversary in November 1915, and Victoria spent the day with
her sisters Margaret and Charlotte while Heinrich and Irene helped to
arrange a quiet celebration. She and Adolf promised one another that they
would celebrate properly after the war was over.

However, that winter Adolf became ill, and began to lose weight to an alarming extent. He had to return home to Bonn on sick leave, and was then sent for treatment in a sanatorium in Godesberg. The doctors assured Victoria that he just needed a period of rest and quiet, but in June his condition worsened and he developed pneumonia. Too badly weakened to recover, he died on 9 July 1916, aged fifty-seven. His body was brought to the palace in Bonn for a short ceremony of remembrance. The funeral procession left their home through the streets of Bonn for Buckenburg, and after a torchlight procession he was placed in the Mausoleum. The funeral service took place the following day. Most of Victoria's relatives were at the front and unable to attend, but her sister Charlotte came to be with her, as did Adolf's eldest sister Hermine, now Duchess Maximilian of Württemberg, and his sister-in-law Marie Anne, the widowed Hereditary Princess of Schaumburg-Lippe.

Although their marriage had been somewhat colourless and frustrated by disappointments, Victoria and Adolf had remained devoted to each other. Despite the court gossip about Victoria's ready eye for handsome young men, there is no evidence to suggest that she ever had any serious affairs, and she was left bereft at the loss of her 'gentle, chivalrous and most unselfish'[5] husband. Aged fifty at the time of her widowhood, she became more solitary and withdrew into herself.

As the war went on, food shortages were becoming acute. Even as a princess, Victoria was subject to a certain amount of deprivations. The naval blockade of Germany was making food harder to obtain, and what was available was of increasingly poor quality. As cattle had no proper food and had to be killed half-grown, meat was bad, the cows produced less milk, and what there was had to be reserved for babies, the elderly, and sick. Farmers were not allowed to feed their hens with corn, so they did not lay and there were therefore no eggs, only a variety of unpleasant egg substitutes. Rye bread might be baked from whatever ingredients were to hand, even sawdust and straw. Corn coffee replaced real coffee, and tea was replaced by a foul-tasting brew made from strawberry and blackberry leaves. There was no leather with which to make new shoes or boots, and women had to go without stockings. As such shortages and other hardships intensified, unrest in the major cities increased, accompanied by rumours of mass disaffection in the army.

In the autumn of 1917, Victoria visited her aunt Louise, Dowager Grand Duchess of Baden, in her palace at Karlsruhe. Relations between them, now both widowed, had not always been harmonious. During her father's lifetime, Louise had been one of the fiercest opponents of her niece's plans to marry the Prince of Bulgaria, yet over the years all had been forgiven and forgotten. Karlsruhe had suffered from French bombing raids in June 1915 and 1916, with much loss of life on both occasions. The very first thing Victoria was shown on her arrival was the way to the cellar, for shelter in case of another raid. When she visited Karlsruhe, she was astonished to see that the number of windows left broken and unrepaired after the explosions easily outnumbered those which were still whole.[6]

During the winter of 1917-18, Daisy, Princess of Pless, invited Victoria, Margaret, her husband, and their two youngest sons, to stay with her at Berchtesgaden, her home in Bavaria. For the sisters and other relations, it made a pleasant break with the boredom and sadness they had experienced since the outbreak of war; the time passed cheerfully with several sledge parties. There was one occasion for anxiety when they went out and totally lost sight of Daisy for a while. They searched for her in vain, and returned to the house, hoping that perhaps she had reached there first. As they did not find her there, a search party was sent out. After darkness fell, a cart drawn by oxen drew up outside the door, and there she sat beside the driver, smiling broadly. She explained that she had indeed lost her way, and a local man had found her and brought her home. But she could not help admitting she had had a really lovely time, and found it such an adventure out of the ordinary.[7]

The war was taking its toll of the family. Margaret had lost two of her sons in action, while Victoria carried on as best she could by helping the wounded, supporting war charities, and lending her car to help transport casualties from the railway station at Bonn to the city hospitals. Princess Daisy of Pless saw her at this time, and although they only spent fifteen minutes together, she noted the loneliness in her.

In Greece, Queen Sophie was soon to find herself an unfortunate victim of Entente propaganda. Soon after the outbreak of war, Kaiser Wilhelm begged King Constantine not to throw in his lot with 'the Serbian assassins', and to bring Greece into the conflict on the side of the Central Powers. Convinced that neutrality was the best stance for his country, the King refused to join either side in the war. However, his training at the Military Academy in Berlin, his visit to his imperial brother-in-law in Berlin shortly after his accession—at which he had been obliged to don a German field marshal's uniform– and his Chief of Staff Ioannis Metaxas's training and education in Germany, all fuelled the suspicion that he was pro-German at heart. Not long after the outbreak of war, the Allied and Central Powers were both exerting pressure on King Constantine to support their cause. The former asserted that he was pro-German, and that Queen Sophie, the Kaiser's brother, must be even more so. Unpleasant rumours about her reached their peak around the time that Venizelos and the King fell out over Venizelos's insistence on joining the Allies during the Dardanelles campaign.

In the summer of 1915, the King became seriously ill. Pneumonia set in, his condition deteriorated, and two of his ribs had to be removed. It was rumoured that he was not unwell, but that he had been stabbed in the back by the Queen during an argument because he would not allow Greece to join the war on the side of Germany. As his condition deteriorated, an icon bearing the image of the Madonna and Child was brought to him, and when it arrived at the palace people waiting outside for news of his progress knelt and prayed in silence for his recovery. The ailing King himself prayed before the holy image when it was brought to him, and afterwards lapsed into unconsciousness. Within a week, the crisis had passed and he was on the road to recovery. Nevertheless, he would never quite be the same man again.

Although he gradually regained his health, there was no corresponding increase in the popularity of the royal family. The foreign press was quick to suggest that a workshop at Phalerum, the much beloved beach in Athens, contained an apparatus by which submarines could arrive in daylight, remain submerged, and, whilst remaining some distance from the shore, latch onto a pipe that would yield large quantities of oil. Queen Sophie, it was said, would often come to watch this operation in progress. Meanwhile, the German Kaiser's villa at Corfu, the Achilleion, was rumoured to be a submarine base constructed during the years of peace.

In October 1915, M. Denys Cochin, a French minister of state, visited King Constantine. The King declared emphatically that he was not a German; he was Greek through and through, and it was his policy to spare his people from the evils of war. He was also angry over French policy in Greece, and warned the British to watch them carefully in that part of Europe. The British military attaché in Athens informed the Foreign Office in London of what he called the King's tirade against the French, and of the King's declaration that the French were leading the British 'by the nose'. King George V could not agree more; he wrote to his foreign secretary, Sir Edward Grey, that in his view they had allowed France to dictate policy too much, 'and that as a Republic she may be somewhat intolerant of, if not anxious to abolish, the monarchy in Greece'.[8]

Even so, King Constantine and Queen Sophie were in a difficult position, one from which they were fortunate to escape unscathed. They had close personal friends among the British. One was Admiral Mark Kerr, who had lived in Greece for some years, and was Commander-in-Chief of the Royal Hellenic Navy and thus chief naval adviser to King Constantine. He considered that the King had a great strategic and tactical brain for war, was truthful through and through, and loathed intrigue—unlike his prime minister Venizelos—but unfortunately was no diplomat and therefore at the mercy of those who were more devious than himself. The other was

Lord Kitchener, British Secretary of State for War, who visited Athens in the autumn of 1915 to assess the internal situation for himself. He and the King immediately liked and respected each other, and Kitchener agreed that, under the circumstances, neutrality was the stance best suited to national interests, and the interests of the Allies would be best served by a continuation of Greece's 'benevolent neutrality'. Sadly for the King and Queen, Kitchener was lost at sea in June 1916 when the armoured cruiser HMS *Hampshire*, on which he was travelling on a diplomatic mission to Russia, was struck by a mine. His successor as minister for war was David Lloyd George, a great admirer of Venizelos, but not of King Constantine.

Margaret became increasingly concerned for Sophie, telling Lady Corkran that 'you can imagine how much I worry about my sister and the horrible position they are in'.[9] Before long, the country was bitterly divided into two factions, one supporting Venizelos, the other the King. After Allied troops entrenched themselves in the city of Salonika, Venizelos established a provisional government there as a rival administration to that of the King in Athens. When one of the King's brothers, Christopher, visited Russia and met Empress Alexandra, the latter was furious with the Allies for their policy regarding Greece. England and France, she wrote to Tsar Nicholas, were 'at the bottom of it', and she feared that, thanks to their actions, a revolution was now pending.[10] Ironically, she seemed more clear-sighted about affairs in Greece than at home in Russia, where her partisanship of the peasant Rasputin and her interference in government appointments were undermining her husband's throne. Meanwhile, another of the King's brothers, Andrew, visited London, only to be asked coldly by an official at the Foreign Office what reception he might be expecting given that his Queen was the sister of the German Kaiser. Nobody had the right, Andrew retorted, to ruin a country simply on account of the relatives of its Queen.

Just before dawn in the early hours of 14 July 1916, a distant wall of fire was seen creeping towards the royal family's estate at Tatoi. The King and Queen saw the flames coming nearer as the wind blew them through the tinder-dry trees at an alarming pace. In their rush to escape, the King tripped over a tree root and sprained his ankle; two soldiers had to carry him to safety just before their path was sealed off by the flames. Queen Sophie and their youngest child, three-year-old Katherine, became separated from other members of the group by the smoke and were also almost trapped. With the child in her arms, she ran for almost two miles to safety, almost fainting from sheer exhaustion once they were clear. Eighteen men were killed in the inferno, the bodies of some charred beyond identification, as well as a large number of animals. While investigating the next day, the police discovered three empty petrol cans at different points in the forest.

By the autumn of 1916, King Constantine's position was becoming ever less tenable. In November, Venizelos overruled him and declared war on the Central Powers. Early the next month, detachments of French and British marines disembarked on the Greek coast and marched on Athens. After several hours of bombardment and firing, there were heavy casualties on both sides. The King and Queen were in the palace with two of their daughters; the Queen was hiding in the cellar with young Katherine and the women servants. At length the Allies withdrew their troops, but even so they conferred official recognition on the government of Venizelos.

Matters went from bad to worse when the ports were blockaded and the Russian revolution overthrew Tsar Nicholas—he had been the royal couple's most ardent defender. By now the King and Queen were almost ready to consider throwing in their lot with Germany, which after all had not attacked Greece, unlike the Allies, who had undermined their position. The Queen told the German Kaiser how desperate their situation was. She sent telegrams enquiring when the German armies would be ready for a definite offensive in Macedonia, as they alone would have the power to deliver Greece from a dire situation made more hopeless by a lack of provisions and munitions and the pressure of the Allied blockade. As the King's brother would later write, if a person's house is broken into, plundered and set fire to 'by persons whom you consider to be your best friends, have the latter any right to call you a "traitor" because, in despair, you opened your window and screamed for help?'[11]

However, by this time it was too late, and the formation of a new government by Alexander Zaimis could likewise do nothing to improve matters. For Margaret and Sophie, who had always been so close, and had regularly visited each other and stayed together at Eastbourne nearly every summer since their mother's death, this was a harsh new world order. 'Too cruel & too senseless,' Margaret wrote despairingly in May 1917 to her friend. 'You can imagine what it means to us both. Soon we shall have been separated 3 years.'[12]

The following month, Charles Jonnart, Allied High Commissioner, informed King Constantine that the Allies were demanding his abdication on the grounds that he had violated his oath as a constitutional monarch. He must renounce the throne and leave the country immediately, otherwise Athens would be attacked again and the dynasty driven out of Greece for the foreseeable future. King Constantine would not risk propelling the country into civil war and further bloodshed.

Because he had served in the German army before the war, Crown Prince George was deemed unacceptable as a successor. Reluctantly, King Constantine appointed their second son Alexander as King in his stead, with the understanding that after the war was over, Constantine would return to Greece as a ruling sovereign. For a while crowds surrounded the palace, determined that the royal family should not be driven out. The King, Queen, and their immediate family tried to leave by car through a side entrance, but a group of guardsmen supposedly threw themselves on the ground in front in an attempt to stop the vehicle. At length, they found that the only way they could leave was through a different entrance, where they were bundled quickly into waiting cars before the crowds realised who they were. As they departed for an indefinite period of exile in neutral Switzerland, Sophie and Constantine left behind an Athens deep in mourning; banks, shops and theatres closed, and the people were astonished that their King and Queen could be disposed of so unceremoniously.

Just as one sister had effectively lost her crown, albeit temporarily, for a while it seemed the youngest might assume one herself. After the Russian revolution in December 1917, the former Grand Duchy of Finland proclaimed its independence. Monarchists were in a minority in the Finnish Parliament, and the state was declared a republic. In January 1918, war broke out between the forces of the Social Democrats led by the People's Deputation of Finland, the 'Reds', supported by the Russian Soviet Republic, and the forces of the conservative-led Senate, the 'Whites', assisted by German forces. A workers' revolt against the first government was put down with the intervention of German troops, and after four months of fighting in which about 37,000 people were killed, peace was declared in May 1918. Plans for a constitutional monarchy were made for Finland, which now had close ties to the German Empire, the only international power to have supported its hopes for independence, and the Senate determined to establish a separate kingdom. The leaders consulted Kaiser Wilhelm, who recommended Prince Friedrich Karl as a suitable candidate. The Finnish leaders still had faith in German victory in the war, and they thought that such a close alliance to the empire would be a guarantee of protection by German troops from another Bolshevik uprising. An initial approach was made to Friedrich Karl on 5 September. Before a new constitution could be adopted, he was elected to the throne on 9 October, an honour to which he reluctantly agreed. His monarchical designation would be Väinö I, King of Finland and Karelia, Duke of Aland, Grand Duke of Lapland, Lord of Kaleva and the North. Later that month, he called his sons home to discuss their future as the royal family of Finland. Philipp was to remain in Germany to succeed his father as head of the family in Hesse, while Wolfgang would become Crown Prince of the new state. Meanwhile, Friedrich Karl prepared himself for the role of sovereign-elect by learning the language with Finnish tutors, and reading up on the country and its people.

However, by September 1918, it was clear that Germany had no alternative to conceding defeat in the war. The Finnish government of Prime Minister Lauri Ingman, a staunch monarchist, was advised that a German King would be untenable, particularly in view of suspicion that the Germans planned to dominate Eastern Europe. This would undermine any hope for peace negotiations, especially in view of the role which the anti-monarchical Woodrow Wilson, President of the United States, intended to assume in the process. Meanwhile, the foreign offices in London and Paris wrote that while they had no objection to the Finnish people choosing a monarch, they would not recognise Kaiser Wilhelm's brother-in-law on the throne.

With the imminent collapse of Germany's allies, the war was lost and she was obliged to seek peace. The Allied Powers would only consider terms that acknowledged their total victory, and Wilson insisted that the destruction of arbitrary power under the German Kaiser was non-negotiable. A naval mutiny broke out at Kiel on 4 November, and troops which had pledged their imperial allegiance were loyal no more. Faced with the possibility of anarchy and civil war, the Kaiser was advised to abdicate. At first he tried to insist that he would step down as German Kaiser but remain King of Prussia, but in vain; his renunciation of the throne was proclaimed by his second cousin Prince Max of Baden, the Imperial Chancellor, the man who once might have become his sister Margaret's husband. As Wilhelm left his country for exile in Holland, a republic was proclaimed and that week the armistice was signed. Europe was once again at peace. The Kaiser and the Empress initially settled in Amerongen Castle, where on 28 November he signed a formal statement of abdication as Kaiser and King, and released his soldiers and officials from their oath of loyalty. It was the end of 400 years of Hohenzollern rule over Prussia. Within two years he had bought a property at nearby Doorn, where he would spend the rest of his life.

Friedrich Karl and Margaret had not embraced the prospect of becoming King and Queen of Finland with enthusiasm. By December 1918, the issue was formally closed, and they could resume their quiet existence as private citizens at Friedrichshof.

The closing months of 1918 remained a period of strain for the family. Margaret and Friedrich Karl were still grieving for their two eldest sons, and they had had the uncertainty of the Finnish proposal. Some of the Allies were demanding the former Kaiser's trial as a war criminal, although Dutch law prohibited the extradition of aliens seeking political refuge. Sophie was in exile with an ailing husband and young children, likewise facing an uncertain future. Finally, the murder of one of their cousins, the former Empress Alexandra of Russia, and her family in captivity only a few months earlier had horrified sovereigns throughout Europe.

Even though Margaret, Friedrich Karl, and their sons were not a ruling family, they still feared the revolutionaries. Soldiers from occupying forces requisitioned their car, horses, and wagons without warning, and drove them around the area waving red banners. The family never recovered their property. Representatives of the workers' and soldiers' councils arrived at Kronberg, making demands including billeting insurgents in the castle and the stables. Sergeant Koch of the 81st Regiment arrived at their breakfast table one morning and told them that murder threats had been made against each member of the family. He wanted to escort them somewhere less dangerous, but they insisted that they would not go. Nevertheless it was unsettling to be informed by loyal friends and servants that revolutionary units could be outside their door—or even trying to break in—at any time. Friedrich Karl contemplated moving them to another of their properties, but on consideration, chose only to move precious documents and valuables. Wolfgang went to address troops in Frankfurt, whom he thought would be loyal to the family, and asked them whether they were prepared to come to Friedrichshof to help protect them. When told abruptly by one officer that they were 'not here to guard castles', he responded that it was not a matter of castles, but people's lives.[13] As he could not find anybody there willing to help, he went to see the head of one of the revolutionary groups which had made themselves a base in a local hotel. At first he was subjected to threats until it was pointed out to one of the leaders, a former sailor, that Prince Friedrich Karl had always been held in high esteem by the troops of the 81st Regiment. Nevertheless, he was warned that he and his family could not expect any preferential treatment.

In the end the family were unharmed, and little property was forcibly taken from them, but the anxiety of those few weeks left its mark. In January 1919, an American senator and a group of officers arrived at Amerongen carrying a letter from the US government. The senator intended to take the former Kaiser and deliver him to the American army on the Rhine. They were led away by the police.[14] There were similar attempts and rumours of efforts to remove the exiled ruler and his consort, and his closest relatives knew they were also in peril. Over the next few years, their dread of 'the red menace' and those whom they suspected of Bolshevik sympathies would be instrumental in persuading Margaret, her husband, and her family to place their faith in the opposing faction. They would ultimately regard the Nazis as a safeguard in helping to protect them and their rights, as well as being the political organisation that would surely restore Germany to her former greatness.

7

'They would show us who the masters were'
1919–26

Although the war was officially over, for Margaret, Friedrich Karl and their sons, the conflict continued. In December 1918, French troops moved into the Rhineland; their arrival did, at least, disband the revolutionary workers' and soldiers' councils at Kronberg. Nevertheless, the occupying forces were quick to impose new restrictions on the personal liberty of locals. French troops dictated that an exclusive pass was needed to enter or leave the *Brückenköpf* (bridgehead), which effectively cut off those who lived at Friedrichshof from Frankfurt.

In June 1919 a contingent of French soldiers broke into Friedrichshof, took over the private suite of rooms which had been used by the Empress Frederick, and banished the family to a cottage in the grounds. As Friedrich Karl noted angrily in his diary, 'they repeated over and over that they would show us who the masters were'.[1] To add insult to injury, the troops stationed military equipment throughout the park in what was meant to be a clear demonstration of force by the victorious side. After the German government had ratified the Treaty of Versailles, the French evacuated the building but kept the bridgehead until 1930. Margaret, Friedrich Karl, and their sons deeply resented this humiliation, whilst Philipp became firmly convinced that the French soldiers were intercepting his letters. He wrote to his friend, the poet Siegfried Sassoon, that it would not surprise him to learn that they were using them to light their fires.

That same year, Margaret and Friedrich Karl realised that the cost of staffing and maintaining Friedrichshof as they had done in the pre-war period was now beyond their means. They accordingly moved out of the main building and into the house, sometimes called a 'cottage', although in fact it was a reasonably large and very comfortable dwelling, if less grand than a Schloss. The Empress Frederick's rooms were left undisturbed in her memory. Friedrich Karl was an inveterate book collector, and Margaret found it necessary to have a room above the stables converted into a study for him and his library. When Prince Nicholas of Greece, one of King Constantine's brothers, visited them in 1926, he reported that although the great house was closed, it continued to be a shrine of art, belonging to Margaret, 'who has inherited her mother's love for everything beautiful as well as her charm and kindness of heart.'[2]

The previous year, Friedrich Karl had become Landgrave of Hesse-Cassel when his elder brother Alexander renounced the title, and with it he came into possession of Rumpenheim as well as various other properties which belonged to the family. Nevertheless, by now they were comfortably settled at Kronberg and so continued to retain it as their primary home.

Two of Margaret and Friedrich Karl's sons found themselves wives during this decade. In September 1924, Wolfgang married Marie Alexandra of Baden, and the following September his twin brother Philipp married Mafalda of Italy. Queen Margherita, Margaret's godmother, refused to allow a Protestant celebration of the wedding. Margaret and Friedrick Karl were very vexed, and the former Kaiser, already displeased at the prospect of his nephew marrying a Roman Catholic, put pressure on them not to go to Italy to attend the wedding. They accordingly stayed away, with the result that none of Philipp's immediate family were present, although the guests included King Carol of Roumania and his cousin King George II of Greece.

Victoria had faced humiliations of her own in Bonn at the close of the war. She knew that the blockade had made food harder to obtain, and she was probably aware that Germany was facing defeat. Yet as a widow without any children, and presumably only in contact with friends and servants inclined to tell her only what they thought she wanted to hear, she had been somewhat insulated from the everyday course of events. The first time she became fully aware of the deteriorating national situation was a few days before the Kaiser's abdication. One evening, she received an urgent telephone call advising her that she should extinguish all the lights in her house and close the gates, as a crowd of mutinous sailors from the navy at Kiel and other revolutionaries were planning to march on and perhaps even storm the building. They had commandeered a fleet of lorries and were already on their way.

This created panic among Victoria's household and everyone fled to their rooms for safety. Her comptroller, the faithful Herr von Salviati, advised her to leave inconspicuously by the back door before the mob arrived. She proved her courage, telling him that she was not going to run away like a coward and desert her home; she remained in the passage over the entrance hall. Soon they could hear the tramping footsteps of the approaching mob as they entered the park. Within a few seconds the sailors were in her hall, rudely demanding food and drink from the servants, and threatening to smash everything if their requests were not complied with. Victoria had gone to her room upstairs, persuaded to stay out of sight for a while in case her presence irritated them further. Threats were being made against the palace and its occupants, and when she heard some of the ringleaders threaten to shoot Salviati if he did not satisfy their demands, she decided to face them herself.

Her maid Clara Franz begged her not to expose herself to any danger, caught her skirt and tried to hold her back, but in vain; Victoria swept past her, went downstairs and asked the men exactly what they wanted. First they asked her for cigarettes, which she gave them, noting with some satisfaction that they did not attempt to light them in her presence. Then they demanded that she should hand her car over to them. She agreed that they could borrow it, but only on condition that it was returned by 9.30 the following morning, as she would need it for taking the wounded to hospital. At this they stood to attention, saluted and informed her respectfully that they were Prussian soldiers and would keep their word. Her car, they promised, would be sent back early in the morning.[3] To her surprise, they kept their promise. In the morning it was returned, having been used throughout the night to take convicts which they had liberated from the city gaols. That said, it was noticed that the crown had been removed and the monogram scratched off. A few days later, the armistice was declared.

With the final defeat of the German army and the abdication and withdrawal of the Kaiser to Holland, revolution broke out in Germany. As troops left the front, Victoria had to accommodate Lt-Gen. Otto von Below and his staff, and as many of his men as possible. For a while she had about sixty horses and the men camped in her small riding school.

The regiments which had been garrisoned at Bonn for much of the war departed just before the army of occupation arrived. Canadian troops occupied Bonn in December, and for the citizens and their princess, it was a most humiliating moment. As the Canadians marched into the town, the streets were vacated, all blinds were pulled down and shutters were closed. Lieutenant-General Arthur Currie, commander of the Canadian Expeditionary Force in Europe, and his staff found it necessary to requisition one wing of the palace for their own use. The situation was initially complicated by the fact that Victoria and her staff were in effect living in a military camp. Many restrictions and difficulties were imposed upon them, and identity cards were required for all who entered the palace. She was forbidden to ride beyond the limits of the park, and while the soldiers were there she constantly worried about damages to the building and the safety of her treasured possessions.

Around Christmas 1918, Prince Albert, the second son of King George V, came to visit Lieutenant-General Currie. When he met Victoria for the first time, he was astonished by her ignorance of the atrocities committed by her countrymen, and their treatment of prisoners of war during the conflict. He wrote to his father on New Year's Day 1919 that she seemed to have very little idea of what her British cousins' feelings now were towards Germany. His equerry Louis Greig told her about some of his experiences as a prisoner, and this was the first indication she had of what wartime conditions had really been like. Yet she was unable to grasp how high feelings ran as she asked after the family, and expressed a perhaps natural hope that they all would rekindle their friendships again shortly. The prince told her politely that he did not think it possible for a great many years. She then told him that her brother had never wanted the war, any Zeppelin raids on England or even any U-boats, but Greig interpreted that as 'only a ruse to get friendly with us'. The King replied that he was quite correct to do so. 'The sooner she knows the real feeling of bitterness which exists here against her country the better.'[4]

At around the same time, the prince's elder brother Edward, Prince of Wales, was also billeted to the palace. He was annoyed to find photographs of his family displayed in several of the rooms, and when he wrote to Queen Mary, he admitted that the sight of them made him feel ashamed; his only consolation was the thought that 'we've "cut them right out" for ever!' Victoria inadvertently added to his feelings of irritation when they met by addressing him as 'dear'—she was twenty-eight years younger than him—and told him that Germany would have been able to continue the war for several years had it not been for the revolution. Although he protested fiercely against the Germans as a race, he conceded reluctantly, if a little oddly, that this German second cousin seemed 'a nice enough woman for a Hun,' as she was after all one-third English.[5]

Victoria's sole surviving uncle would prove more accommodating. Four months later in May 1919, Arthur, Duke of Connaught, came to inspect the troops in Bonn. Despite what King George may have thought or said to the contrary, the Duke expressed a wish to see his niece. It proved to be a short meeting, since in her words he was 'very pressed for time', or might have thought it diplomatic to avoid making more than a token gesture. Yet the time he was prepared to spend with her 'was just sufficient to talk over bygone days, and he was, as usual, most affectionate'.[6] It was probably the last time that she would ever see or even have contact with any of her British relations.

As part of the Schaumburg Palace was used by the occupying forces until 1926, it was a relief for Victoria to get away and renew contacts with those relatives and friends still prepared to talk to her. The coming of the German republic had to an extent liberated her from some of the constraints and trouble of living a semi-public life. She was keenly aware of the depression and humiliation suffered by her eldest brother the Kaiser, now living in Doorn, Holland, since his abdication. She was also sensitive to the hostility still shown towards her sister Sophie and her family, who now settled in Switzerland. She offered her support to both of them, despite the fact that her brother had not always shown the same kindness towards her. She visited Sophie and encouraged and entertained her children.

When the former Empress Augusta Victoria died in April 1921, aged sixty-two, after a long period of failing health, Victoria demonstrated her forgiving and generous nature in her sympathy for the plight of her lonely brother. His relations with all five of his surviving sons were far from harmonious, and despite regular visits from his children—although his daughter was the only one whose company he really enjoyed—he seemed utterly lost without the Empress. When he fell in love the following year with Hermine, Princess of Schönaich-Carolath, a war widow in her early thirties, and announced his intention to remarry, Victoria was one of the few members of the imperial family magnanimous enough to give unqualified personal support. She, Margaret, and Heinrich were present at their wedding in Doorn that November. Significantly, three of his sons and also his daughter disapproved of the wedding so strongly that they refused to attend. Hermine was Victoria's niece by marriage, and it amused them that Victoria's eldest brother was now also her nephew.

It was the only visit Victoria ever paid to Doorn, and she recalled how Heinrich came to collect her at the station in his car and her happy meeting with Wilhelm; they had not met for some time, 'and there was much to talk over'.[7] She was probably blissfully unaware that she did not make a favourable impression on her brother or his guests. He evidently held strict views about women trying to keep the natural ageing process at bay with cosmetics, and commented afterwards with great disapproval on 'her sharp face utterly covered in thick powder', which he thought 'quite dreadful'. His physician Dr Alfred Haehner was even more scathing about her appearance, noting in his diary that her way of life 'was written clearly on her face for all to see', and it was as if one had come 'face to face with the madame of a brothel'.[8]

The death of the Empress was not the only bereavement the family experienced in the post-war years. On 1 October 1919, Charlotte, Hereditary Princess of Saxe-Meiningen, lost her battle with ill-health. Only fifty-nine, she had suffered from porphyria, the condition of which her great-great-grandfather King George III had been the most notable victim. 'My sister's death was quite an unexpected loss,' Margaret wrote to

Above left: Wilhelm I, King of Prussia from 1861, created German Emperor in 1871.

Above right: Queen Victoria and Queen Augusta at Frogmore, 1867.

Above left: Crown Prince Friedrich Wilhelm, about 1880.

Above right: Victoria, Princess Royal, 1856, shortly after her betrothal to Prince Friedrich Wilhelm.

Above left: The German Crown Prince and Princess with their six children at Neue Palais, Potsdam, 1875.

Above right: Princesses Sophie, Victoria and Margaret with their brother Prince Waldemar, June 1878. (*Royal Collection Trust/Copyright Her Majesty Queen Elizabeth II 2014*)

Princesses Sophie and Margaret, *c.* 1887.

An artist's impression of Prince Alexander of Battenberg abdicating as Prince of Bulgaria at gunpoint, surrounded by Russian soldiers, August 1886.

Above left: Crown Prince Friedrich Wilhelm preparing to take part in Queen Victoria's Jubilee procession, June 1887.

Above right: 'Bismarck forbids the banns!' *Punch,* 14 April 1888, Linley Sambourne's comment on Bismarck's attitude to a marriage between Princess Victoria and Prince Alexander of Battenberg.

Queen Victoria with the Prince and Princess of Wales, around the time of the Queen's Jubilee in June 1887.

Princesses Victoria, Sophie and Margaret taking a morning ride at Charlottenburg, 1888.

Above: The wedding of Princess
Margaret of Prussia and Prince
Friedrich Charles of Hesse-Cassel,
January 1893, with the bride's mother,
Empress Friedrich, on the right.

Right: The performance of the
Fackeltanz or torch dance at the
wedding celebrations of Princess
Margaret of Prussia and Prince
Friedrich Charles of Hesse-Cassel.

Above left: The Empress Friedrich during the early years of her widowhood.

Above right: Princess Friedrich Karl of Hesse-Cassel with her two elder sons, Princes Friedrich Wilhelm and Maximilian.

The Empress Friedrich's home, Friedrichshof, north side and main entrance.

Two family groups taken at Friedrichshof on 24 May 1900, Queen Victoria's 81st birthday.

Above: Crown Princess Sophie of Greece; Princess Adolf of Schaumburg-Lippe; Emperor Wilhelm II; their mother the Empress Friedrich; Charlotte, Hereditary Princess of Saxe-Meiningen; Prince Heinrich; Princess Friedrich Charles of Hesse-Cassel.

Below: a larger group, also including the Crown Princess's elder children, Empress Augusta Victoria, and at the front three of the Empress's sons-in-law and two of her nephews, Prince Albert of Schleswig-Holstein and Ernest, Grand Duke of Hesse and the Rhine.

Above left: Princess Adolf of Schaumburg-Lippe, 1908.

Above right: Queen Sophie of Greece, about the time of her husband's accession as King Constantine, 1913.

Princess Friedrich Charles of Hesse-Cassel in her uniform as Chief of the 80th Fusilier Regiment, *c.* 1910.

Above left: Emperor Wilhelm II.

Above right: Charlotte, Hereditary Princess of Saxe-Meiningen.

Above left: Prince Heinrich.

Above right: Louise, Grand Duchess of Baden, only sister of Emperor Friedrich III.

Prince and Princess Friedrich Charles of Hesse-Cassel, with the Crown Prince and Princess of Greece and their children, 1903. All three young Greek princes, George, Alexander and Paul, were destined to ascend the throne of Greece in later life, while Princess Helen later became Queen Consort of Roumania.

King Edward VII and Emperor Wilhelm II at Homburg, August 1906, with Princess Adolf of Schaumberg-Lippe, Princess Friedrich of Hesse-Cassel, and in the middle Crown Princess Sophie of Greece. (*Royal Collection Trust/Copyright Her Majesty Queen Elizabeth II 2014*)

The Crown Prince and Princess of Greece and their five elder children, 1910. The youngest, Katherine, was born three years later.

Above left: A German postcard of 1911, portraying Emperor Wilhelm II and his siblings.

Above right: Prince and Princess Heinrich, *c.* 1912.

Prince and Princess Friedrich Charles of Hesse-Cassel, with the Crown Prince and Princess of Greece and their children, shortly before the outbreak of the First World War. Within two years Princes Maximilian (right, back row) and Friedrich Wilhelm (right, centre row) would be killed in action.

Above left: Princess Adolf of Schaumburg-Lippe, 1913.

Above right: Emperor Wilhelm II, *c.* 1914

Queen Sophie
with her two
elder daughters,
Princesses Helen
and Irene, *c.* 1921.

King Constantine, Queen Sophie and their family, at around the time of their return to
Greece after the tragic death of their second son, King Alexander, in 1920.

Above left: The former Kaiser Wilhelm II and Margaret, Landgravine of Hesse-Cassel at Doorn, *c.* 1922

Above right: The former Queen Sophie and Ferdinand, former Tsar of Bulgaria, 1923.

Prince Philipp of Hesse-Cassel and his wife Mafalda, daughter of King Victor Emmanuel III of Italy.

Princess Victoria and Alexander Zoubkoff lunching with Bishop Alamatov of the Russian Orthodox Church, immediately prior to their wedding, 21 November 1927.

The former Queen Sophie, Margaret, Landgravine of Hesse-Cassel, and their children, *c.* 1928.

Alexander Zoubkoff and his
wife, the former Princess Victoria
of Prussia and Princess Adolf of
Schaumburg-Lippe, February 1928,
at a press reception at which they
just announced plans for a flight
to America, one of Zoubkoff's
schemes which never took place.

The Landgravine of Hesse-Cassel,
the youngest and last surviving
member of the family, 1946.

Lady Corkran, 'I had no idea how ill she was, & she evidently thank God did not know it herself, for she was still full of plans, & never alluded to anything in her letters. She must have suffered agonies, & one can but be grateful that she was spared more pain, & that the end came so quickly & peacefully.'[9] Her life had not been made any happier by her wretched relationship with her husband Bernhard on the one hand, and their only child and son-in-law, Prince and Princess Heinrich of Reuss, on the other. The aunts of the former Princess Feodora had been greatly saddened by the bitterness between her and her parents and had several times tried to make peace, as had her easy-going uncle Heinrich and his wife Irene, but to no avail.

The exiled Greek royal family in Switzerland took up residence in November 1919 at the Hotel National, Lucerne. Sophie declared that she wanted to try to lead as normal a life as possible, being just like any other guest: no longer a Queen, but just an ordinary human being. It could be that she envied her brother in the Netherlands, an exile who had had his responsibilities removed from him and was now living out his days in peace and comfort as a private citizen. She, on the other hand, had two major crosses to bear. One was the separation from her son Alexander, who, against his own wishes and without preparation for the throne, had been made King in his father's place. The other was the humiliation of being cold-shouldered by old friends, especially the English. She was particularly upset when a group of hotel acquaintances from whom she had accepted invitations to dine before the war cut her and her husband dead, leaving any room that she and the King entered without a word. Only when she learned what some English newspapers were printing about her did she discover why.

Another incident which caused Sophie and her husband significant consternation was Alexander's engagement. He had lost his heart to Aspasia Manos, daughter of one of the royal equerries, Colonel Petros Manos. Although she was descended from a perfectly acceptable Greek family, it was considered that having a native of the country marrying into the ruling dynasty would cause problems. As opposition to the romance grew in Greece, it was alleged that members of Aspasia's family would be certain to try to wield power once she became the King's consort. A rumour surfaced that her father had been forced to commit suicide because of a scandal connected with the King's elder sister Helen. Queen Sophie wrote to Alexander, imploring him not to persist with the match, lest it cause Constantine more stress and lead to a further breakdown in his health. In this, at least, they were in complete agreement with Venizelos. Given that Alexander was miserable as King, completely isolated from members of his family, surrounded by spies and distressed by the constant propaganda levelled against his parents, he became determined to find what happiness and company he could. Only a wife, and one whom he had chosen for himself, could make life tolerable. He had an ally in his great-uncle Arthur, Duke of Connaught, who had been sent to Athens by King George V to confer the Grand Cross of the Order of the Bath on the young monarch. There Arthur met Aspasia Manos, was particularly impressed with her, and told the lonely young bachelor accordingly.

In spite of popular feeling and the reservations of his parents, the King decided to marry Aspasia, and in November 1919 they had a private wedding in a secret Orthodox ceremony. The general reaction in Greece was so hostile that when the news emerged, Aspasia was forced to leave the country. She fled to Rome and then to Paris, where Venizelos allowed the King to join her on an official visit in May 1920. Aspasia was permitted to accompany her husband wherever he went, as long as she did not take part in any formal events where she might be treated as a Queen.

Queen Sophie was delighted to hear that her son was going to travel abroad, especially as she believed that this would at last give her an opportunity to speak to him on the telephone. For some days she could talk of little else but the chance to make proper contact once again with her son. However, when she tried to call him while he was in Paris, the Greek minister answered curtly with the information that His Majesty was sorry, but was unable to come to the telephone. According to her brother-in-law Christopher, the disappointment evident in her reaction 'wrung one's heart'.[10] In fact, Alexander was quite unaware of it, and was never informed that his mother had been making efforts to get in touch with him. As a result, she redoubled her efforts to follow news of him and his movements as closely as possible, cutting out every reference to his activities in the newspapers, and seeking out anybody who had, if only briefly, seen him.

When the couple returned to Greece the marriage was legalized, but regarded as morganatic, therefore the now pregnant Aspasia was given the title of Madame Manos. Their life together would not outlast the year. In October 1920, King Alexander was walking his German shepherd dog when it was attacked by a pet monkey, and in trying to separate the animals he was bitten on the leg. At first he made light of his wounds, and they were cleaned and dressed but not cauterized. Septicaemia set in, and he became delirious. King Constantine and Queen Sophie were warned that his life was in some danger, and she begged to be allowed to travel back to Greece and visit him for what she knew would surely be the last time, but the Greek government was fearful of pro-royalist demonstrations and refused to allow her in. Frantic with despair, she then begged Queen

Olga to try to obtain permission to go to him so that he should see at least one member of his family before the end. Her request was granted, but the Dowager's journey was delayed by stormy weather. By the time she reached Athens, the twenty-seven-year-old King lay dead.

Queen Sophie and King Constantine were distraught at the news and Margaret, who had known what it was like to lose two beloved sons, made the journey to Lucerne to comfort her sister. Having lost two sons herself, she sympathized greatly with Sophie's pain. She wrote to Lady Corkran having spent three weeks in Sophie's company, and reported that she was heartbroken:

> [She] & will never get over this loss, it was all so cruel.—It will be a great thing if they can return & the loyalty of the people is of course a great help, but what it will mean to her to go back & see the empty house & to think of all her poor boy suffered during those lonely years is terrible to imagine.[11]

It was an abiding sorrow which she never completely got over.

From his exile at St Cloud, Paris, King Constantine's brother George had written to Grand Duchess Xenia of Russia, sister of the late Tsar Nicholas II, about the generally distressing state of affairs throughout Europe from the Greek royal family's point of view:

> Morals, principals [sic], heart and every Christian feeling has been done away with by this infernal war and those who are guiding the nation today are all without religion.... Yes poor Sophie has been forbidden to go and see her poor dying son who in his delirium was constantly calling for his mother. It's hard to realise that people can have so little heart.[12]

The following month, new elections in Greece resulted in defeat for Venizelos and he too went into exile. In December 1920, a plebiscite was held to ask the people whether they wanted King Constantine to return. The result was a decisive victory for him, with over ten million votes in his favour and less than 11,000 cast against him. On 19 December, the royal family returned to scenes of extraordinary enthusiasm in the streets around the palace. Although pleased and relieved to be back, the family were not deceived as to their own true feelings, in particular those of the Queen, still in deep mourning for her son. Prince Christopher watched her smiling at the cheering crowds, only to see that 'her heart bled in secret'.[13]

Shortly after their return to Athens, two marriage alliances were brokered between the Greek and Roumanian royal families, the latter being the children of Queen Sophie's first cousin Queen Marie and King

Ferdinand. Crown Prince George of Greece became engaged to Princess Elisabetha, and Helen to Crown Prince Carol. Being well aware of the unpleasant characters of her Roumanian niece and nephew, Queen Sophie struggled to raise much enthusiasm about either match. In particular, she feared losing her daughter to a prince who was known to be besotted with another woman. Nevertheless, Elisabetha and George were married in Bucharest on 27 February, and Carol and Helen in Athens on 10 March 1921. Shortly before the wedding, Margaret would confide to Lady Corkran that her sister had shown much courage in 'fighting down her grief & working for others. It will be terrible for her to give up that daughter she adores & she dreads it.'[14]

While she was at the wedding, Queen Sophie was distraught at finding herself snubbed by more Englishmen whom she and King Constantine had previously regarded as close friends. This presented a grim contrast to the spontaneous affection with which they had been greeted by the Athenians, on whom the Allied Powers, encouraged by the French, had been quick to turn their backs on. Lord Curzon warned Lord Granville, former official British minister in Athens, that they should remain in Athens but avoid all ceremonial, official, and personal relations with King Constantine, his court, and his family. Lord and Lady Granville greeted Queen Marie of Roumania cordially, but pointedly ignored the King and Queen.

After the wedding, Constantine and Sophie's next concern was the unfinished business regarding Greece's campaign to reclaim her historic rights over Constantinople, and to rescue the Greeks who had been living under the Turkish yoke. While still in power, Venizelos had aligned the country with the Allied side in time for Greece to be authorized at the Paris Peace Conference in 1919 to occupy the town of Smyrna, a lifeline to the Turks with a large Greek population. Greek troops had pushed Turkish forces back, but after King Constantine's restoration to the throne, the Allies rescinded their promises of armed support. The French government justified its withdrawal with the escalating cost of maintaining a zone of occupation in Asia Minor and its desire to make peace with Turkey. King Constantine thus found himself persisting in a war where the chances of victory now looked extremely slender. Several years earlier, he had warned Venizelos that an invasion of Asia Minor would surely result in Greece's destruction, yet as the population demanded it, he had no choice but to continue the military campaign.

King Constantine, who was still in poor health, took command of his forces, while Queen Sophie once again assisted nursing the wounded at the field hospitals. Lacking allies, the Greeks were heavily outnumbered and soon driven back. Margaret came to stay with her sister in May 1922 and was shocked at the state of her: 'the heat tries her terribly, & all she has been through tells on her naturally.'[15] What she needed, her sister believed, was a complete change and period of rest at Friedrichshof, but there was no question of that until peace was signed and affairs were more settled.

After a few weeks, the Greek war effort was exhausted; peace negotiations were instigated, and King Constantine's abdication was demanded by the army. In September 1922, he and Queen Sophie left Greece for what they knew would be the last time, and settled in Palermo, Sicily. On 11 January 1923, they were on the point of moving from their hotel to Florence when the broken King, whose health had further deteriorated, collapsed with a massive cerebral haemorrhage and died, aged fifty-four. His body was taken to Naples for a funeral service in the Greek Church, and from there to the Russian Church at Florence, where it was laid to rest in the crypt. Their son King George was not even able to allow his father's body to be returned to Greece for burial.

Now an impoverished widow and exile, Queen Sophie's plight touched many members of her family and her friends. Infanta Eulalia remarked that she was 'one of the best of women; her patience in adversity was wonderful, and her stoical philosophy enabled her to regard her life entirely as a state of *omnia veritas*, in which nothing was lasting.'[16] Yet not everybody had been quite as sympathetic to her situation. A Mrs Whitaker, one of the members of English society in Sicily who met King Constantine and Queen Sophie about two months before the King's sudden death, commented with asperity on how their ministers in Greece had been tried on charges of treason by the new regime, found guilty, and been executed. Constantine's youngest brother Andrew, whose wife Alice had recently given birth to a son, Philip, was also charged with military incompetence during the war, sentenced to death, and was only saved at the last minute after a personal appeal from King George V of Great Britain. While this was happening, wrote Mrs Whitaker, the exiled sovereigns were in Palermo, 'accepting little tea parties and going to the motor races, in three cars.' The Queen, she noted, had 'large grey-blue, very sad and patient eyes'. Her husband seemed 'stunned, or more likely indifferent', and his main outside interest appeared to be 'watching the vulgar dancing at the Villa Igica'.[17]

For several years after the war, Victoria's life 'progressed very quietly', according to her memoirs.[18] She gave occasional tea and dinner parties, rode both the horses she had left, and took daily rides with her groom. During the summer she played tennis, and began to take singing lessons which went on throughout the year. However, like other royals of the age, her finances were badly affected by post-war inflation and spiralling prices. As a widow she received a monthly allowance of 3,000 marks from the court treasury of Schaumburg-Lippe, although hyper-inflation reduced the value of this sum until it was almost worthless. Moreover, it was her misfortune that the faithful Salviati, who had successfully managed her finances, died at around this time. Her affairs were very complicated; she had never had any experience in managing them herself or any real idea of the value of money. At length she was able to employ the capable Baron von Solemacher, who helped to put her affairs in order. All the same, she was obliged to sell some of her fine pieces of jewellery, valuable furniture, and had to give up her horses and car. From that time onwards, she travelled around Bonn by tram, which conveniently stopped just before her park gates.

Victoria loved cinema, cabaret and nightclubs, as well as the theatre, and was fascinated by new inventions. Despite having been brought up in the nineteenth century, she found that jazz, the rhythm of modern dance bands, and above all the Charleston, appealed enormously to her. Although she was now in her mid-fifties, she still enjoyed dancing for its own sake, and regarded it as first-rate exercise. Herr Stahl, the proprietor of a large cinema near the palace, gave Victoria a permanent entrance card which came with free admission. Although she had to make do on more modest means than previously, she considered herself fortunate that she enjoyed good health and a circle of good friends. Her strong constitution, she believed, was due to her love of the outdoor life since childhood.[19]

A break in what may have been somewhat humdrum routine came in the spring of 1925, when Victoria made a journey to Florence to visit Queen Sophie, now living in exile. She stayed at the Anglo-American Hotel, while her sister was living at Villa Cora, just outside the city. For Victoria, it was a joy to spend some time with Sophie and her daughters Irene and Katherine; they all went sightseeing together like a party of tourists. While she was there, Victoria attended a ceremony at the Russian church where King Constantine had been buried. A small chapel that Sophie had restored was being inaugurated. The service was particularly impressive, and attended by Prince Nicholas and his wife Helen, as well as various Greek friends of Sophie's.

While Victoria was staying there, she took a fancy to a plump baby belonging to one of Sophie's Greek servants, whose wife was also in service. Being very fond of small children in spite of never being able to have any of her own, she made a great fuss of this infant, petting it and carrying it about with her. She admitted that she was 'badly mocked'[20] for doing so, but by this time she had acquired something of a reputation for eccentricity, and this was doubtless accepted as another of her foibles.

In widowhood, Sophie made a new home for herself in Florence with Irene and Katherine. Having seen her husband forced to abdicate not once but twice, she was well aware of the capriciousness of the Greeks. Although Greece was now a republic, she knew that the people might very well summon their royal family back once more as suddenly as they had expelled them; she was therefore reluctant to buy a permanent residence in Florence. This did not prevent her from having her eye on a suitable property *au-cas-où*: a charming fifteenth-century villa near Fiesole, on the wooded hill of San Domenico overlooking the city of Florence. She told Helen that, should their stay become permanent, that was where she would happily live for the rest of her days.

Having members of her family around her for much of the time provided Sophie with some comfort, and in particular she doted on her granddaughter Alexandra, who went to boarding school in Sussex as her aunts had done, and was utterly miserable there. Only regular visits from her mother, who still went to stay in England whenever she could, helped to make the little girl's existence tolerable. Queen Sophie also had the regular companionship of all three daughters for much of the time. The marriage of Helen, the eldest, had fallen apart as a result of her husband Carol's flagrant infidelities and bullying, and they were divorced in 1928. Carol had renounced his place in the order of succession, and on the occasion of his death in 1927, King Ferdinand was accordingly succeeded by Carol and Helen's only child, five-year-old Michael. Three years later, Carol decided he would return to the kingdom he had left, asserted his rights and claimed the throne, reigning until he was driven into exile in 1940.

Queen Sophie was seen at some of the royal gatherings in Europe during the decade, and they would prove a welcome diversion for her. In October 1923, she attended the christening of Crown Prince Peter of Serbia at Belgrade—who would later marry her granddaughter Alexandra—and the wedding of her niece Princess Olga to Prince Paul of Serbia. Her second cousin Albert, Duke of York, later King George VI of Great Britain, told his father that she had 'aged a great deal, poor lady, after all she has been through'.[21] Her ageing became all the more apparent when compared with her cousin Marie, Queen of Roumania, now connected twice again with her through the marriages of their children, who was still full of vitality. The two cousins—Sophie being Marie's elder by only five years—saw much of each other, but in personality and temperament would always be very different. Queen Sophie was invited to one of her homes, Bran Castle, Transylvania, which Marie had decorated in her usual exotic style, the effect being very Byzantine. Queen Sophie's reaction was none too enthusiastic. 'Yes, it's very nice, my dear,' she remarked, 'but at your age?' Marie laughed. 'Yes, my dear, at my age. And I'm not finished yet!'[22]

Queen Marie was always sympathetic to her cousin's ordeal, but found her too defeatist in her outlook. Writing to an American friend in 1936, four years after Sophie had died, she remarked that while she and King Constantine had been treated very unfairly, they both had 'very great limitations'. Sophie, she wrote, was always complaining; 'life seemed for her a weight, a losing battle: her conventionality, her preconceived ideas, tastes and prejudices withered all *joie de vivre* in her. She always felt defeated, so she attracted defeat.' Yet even though Sophie bored her and she felt 'stifled in her company', she admitted that they were still 'quite good friends'.[23]

The British writer Beverley Nichols, who had visited Queen Sophie in Athens shortly before she was forced to leave Greece for the last time, was greatly struck by her appearance. She had, he observed, the saddest face of any woman he had ever seen: 'Standing there, dressed entirely in black, a bowl of lilies by her side, her face rose from the shadows like one who has known every suffering.' Unhappy as she may have been, she was still curious for any details about England which, as she told him, she had not visited since before the war and doubted she ever would set foot in again. As he answered her questions, it dawned on him that 'here was a woman who was sick at heart for the country in which she had played as a child.'[24]

Regardless of being 'sick at heart', Sophie still possessed the knack of being friendly and gracious to friend and foe alike. At one wedding which she attended as a guest in the early years of her widowhood, she found herself sitting next to Ferdinand, former Tsar of Bulgaria, during luncheon. Relations between them had been strained ever since King Constantine and his army had inflicted a crushing defeat on the Bulgarians in 1913, and her brother-in-law Christopher was astonished to see them getting on so well together, seemingly almost inseparable after the meal was over. When Christopher asked her what they had found to talk about, she replied, 'Why, old times, of course,' without a hint of bitterness.[25]

If she had feared for the future of the Greek monarchy as she went into exile, her fears were soon to be realised. Her eldest son George had reigned for only fifteen troubled months before he was faced with little alternative but to leave the kingdom. This time, there was no question of the Greek ministers installing a puppet sovereign to take his place. Instead, they chose to abolish the monarchy, declared the country a republic, and denied all members of the royal family Greek citizenship. It looked like the end of a chapter for Greece.

There were equally happier times ahead of Sophie, especially when she went to stay with Margaret and Friedrich Karl in Germany. Such visits were made livelier by members of the younger generation, for instance when, in the summer of 1926, a tea party hosted by Margaret at Schloss Panker, Holstein, was amusingly ambushed by a herd of pigs set free from their sty by Sophie's granddaughter Alexandra and nephew Philip.[26]

8

'Titles, money, everything may go'
1927–32

In spite of the dire state of her finances in the days of the Weimar Republic, Victoria still had much to be thankful for. Unlike her eldest brother, her sister, and so many other royals of the age, she had not suffered the ignominy of being ordered to leave her own country and her home. Moreover, although widowed, she did not have a family for whom she needed to provide. Even so, when she was invited to write her memoirs for publication sometime during the mid-twenties, she considered the idea a welcome solution to her financial difficulties. The approach was made by a British publisher, Eveleigh, Nash and Grayson. One might well ponder the irony of such an arrangement originating in an Allied country where anti-German feeling still ran high.

As she had always kept a diary, the task did not prove arduous, and the book was completed in 1927. There is no reference in her text to how much help she may have received from an assistant or a biographer, and one can only speculate whether it was mainly her own work, or whether she received substantial editorial assistance.

Victoria writes in the Postscript that, shortly before the work was completed, she found that fate 'had another chapter in store' for her. She was referring to her encounter with Bielskov, a Russian refugee and antique dealer who had assumed the name of Count Ich-Bielskov, in the course of selling some of her possessions. Having bought various precious items from her in the past and maintained contact with her over an extended period, he knew of her generous nature, her general innocence and gullibility, and that she no longer had a husband or any other close family members who lived with or were close to her. It was probably in or around September 1927 that Ich-Bielskov introduced her to a young friend of his, Alexander Zoubkoff. This man, he said, was his cousin and, like himself, he had lost everything in the Bolshevik revolution. Though he had very little money, he was young, handsome, and possessed great charm, not to say cunning, and Victoria became completely spellbound by the richly embellished, if not completely false, accounts he gave her of his adventures and misfortunes.

Zoubkoff was born in 1900 or 1901 in Icanovo, a small village about 6 miles north-east of Odessa where his father owned the village store. He was a master storyteller, and thus any knowledge of him is based largely on what he told others and what he wished them to believe. Two books, one a volume of spurious memoirs, the other in effect an illustrated novel full of gossip and fabricated dialogue purporting to be a biography, and finally a chronicle of misdemeanours which made good copy in the press throughout Europe during the inter-war years, comprise most of what is left to posterity.

As a child he had been clever and resourceful, idle and unscrupulous. After the Russian revolution, he became the favoured boy of the leader of a band of Cossacks, and joined them in robbing local villages and terrorising the Jewish inhabitants. He also developed a taste for cocaine. The victory of the Red Army forced him out of Russia and he spent the next few years in the underworld of Marseilles and Berlin, living off of his wits and on the savings of a succession of prostitutes whom he had befriended. As a refugee he had no papers or official status, and he was perpetually on the run in his efforts to evade the immigration departments of several national police forces throughout Europe. He was well-known to them as a thief and confidence trickster. Some of the women he encountered made efforts to expand his education outside the bedroom with some success, and by the mid-1920s he had learned to assume an aristocratic manner and a veneer of sophistication that added credibility to his claims to noble birth.

The widowed Princess Adolf of Schaumburg-Lippe proved to be an easy target. At the age of sixty, she was still comfortably off, had preserved her good looks and health, and was lonely, still longing for the romance that she felt had always eluded her. She was thoroughly impressed with the good looks, smooth manner and worldliness of the young man. Most of all she related to the life story he recounted to her: that his wealthy aristocratic parents had owned a fine palace; that the family fortune had been largely based on a textile factory; that the revolution had left them penniless; that since leaving Russia he had been forced into providing for himself by taking a succession of menial jobs. He had travelled the world as a deckhand, he said, had sailed to Grimsby and Newcastle, had stayed in England for a few weeks, and in the process had become a fluent English speaker.

The Postscript of her book quoted several extracts from her diary about the progress of their courtship, from their first meeting to the proposal. 'What an interesting young man he is!' was her initial reaction after she invited him and Count Ich-Bielskov to dinner for the first time. She considered him 'tall, dark and handsome' as well as 'very intelligent'. They came to dine again the following evening, and she observed that he danced well, 'but does not care for it'. She invited him to tennis the following morning, and that proved more to his taste. That night he took her to the opera at Cologne, where they enjoyed a performance of Puccini's *Madame Butterfly*. While there, Victoria saw several people whom she knew, but none of them were acquainted with Zoubkoff, and as she perceived it, it was inevitable that they took a great interest in him. The next day, they went boating on the Rhine and enjoyed a picnic in the hills.

A week later she recorded in her diary that she felt herself becoming very fond of 'Sascha', her pet-name for Zoubkoff. When he told her he had to go to Berlin to see his ailing mother who had just arrived from Russia, she confessed that it would seem very dreary and desolate without him. Without a second thought she gave him some money for the journey, and waited anxiously for him to return. This story, like many others, was a fabrication, and he spent the money on drugs, gambling, and prostitutes.

Upon Zoubkoff's return to Bonn, Victoria showered more money and valuables on him. These included suits previously worn by her nephew Crown Prince Wilhelm, watches and personal jewellery belonging to her late husband, and sums to buy residence permits and settle his status. A week after his return from Berlin, she wrote in her diary that she cared for him a great deal and knew that he cared for her. She wondered what people would say to the idea of a marriage between them. A day later, he proposed to her. Overjoyed, she accepted at once.

Naturally, Victoria wondered how her family would react to the news. But she was determined that, in her words, she would 'overstep all barriers'. The last thing she intended to do was to sacrifice her own happiness and that of her fiancé, as she saw it, for the sake of social convention. She was aware that the difference in their ages would be frowned upon, but considered this of lesser importance than her affection. 'Titles, money, everything may go, but I will keep our happiness.'[1]

Later that week, Victoria's brother Heinrich responded to an invitation to come and meet him, as did Sophie and Margaret. Victoria probably cared little of what they thought and, not surprisingly, it proved an uncomfortable occasion for all; nevertheless, she was persuaded that his personality 'soon made them realise that he is indeed a man to be admired'. Their engagement was announced that same night and inevitably made headlines throughout Europe, as an eager press began to delve more assiduously into Zoubkoff's history. While some newspapers expressed horror at the idea of the sixty-one-year-old princess marrying a twenty-seven-year-old Russian charlatan, others did not hesitate to offer backhanded congratulations to the former German Kaiser for having acquired such an interesting brother-in-law. In London, *The Times* formally announced in a brief, six-line paragraph, that the princess 'has become engaged to be married to a Russian émigré, M. Zoubkoff, aged 23 [sic], the scion of a noble Russian family'.[2] Without exception, journalists were fascinated by a German princess, the former Kaiser's sister, marrying a man young enough to be her son and of such unsubstantiated reputation. When she was asked about her forthcoming marriage, Victoria replied that she was seeking to exchange the title of 'princess' for that of a 'happy woman'. Her statement may as well have been political as well as personal, in that she intended to move with the times by making a complete break with her royal life and becoming a private citizen.

Sophie and Margaret both opposed the idea of their sister throwing herself away on a man who was transparently a crook and a wastrel, and they begged her to reconsider her decision. The former Kaiser could take no direct action, barred as he was from entering Germany, yet he still cared enough about Victoria's well-being, or at least the good of the Hohenzollern name, to ask their brother Heinrich to persuade her to call off the engagement. Heinrich tried to no avail, and was told politely but firmly that with regard to such matters, she was no longer prepared to listen to the family. She reasoned that, forty years previously, she had done what they had ordered her to, and in the process had lost her first love, Alexander of Battenberg, Prince of Bulgaria.

A notice was posted at Bonn Registry Office, announcing that the couple planned to marry. The wedding was originally to take place at the end of October, but was delayed because Zoubkoff was officially stateless and had illegally entered Germany. Victoria was advised that her husband-to-be needed to obtain special consent from the authorities in Cologne. Even under the republic, the intervention of a princess still carried some authority, and all the necessary permits were obtained within a few weeks.

Victoria and Zoubkoff were married on 19 November 1927, the thirty-seventh anniversary of her marriage to Adolf, at the Registry Office in Bonn. The newspapers had been full of the impending nuptials, and on the day, crowds had gathered outside the town hall to watch the couple arriving since the dawn. They had wanted a church wedding, but the church in Bonn refused to marry a Protestant bride and Russian Orthodox groom. Zoubkoff accordingly went to a Russian chapel in Wiesbaden, where he found a member of the Russian clergy, Bishop Alamatov, who was prepared to be of service, and drove him back to Bonn. Two days later, Alamatov officiated at a Russian Orthodox wedding ceremony at Schaumburg Palace. It was the anniversary of Empress Frederick's birthday, and Victoria wore her mother's wedding veil over a white bridal gown for the service. The proceedings were witnessed by Baron von Solemacher and Georg, Count von Merenberg, the widower of a daughter of Tsar Alexander II, and his second wife, Catherine, Princess Yourievsky.

In reporting the news from Cologne, a correspondent for *The Times*, which this time more accurately cited the bridegroom's age as twenty-seven, remarked that 'considerable opposition to the marriage has been manifested in some quarters, and it is reported that the former Kaiser has refused to give his consent'.[3] A small reception was held afterwards, at which the groom toasted his wife, Mother Russia and the Tsar— presumably the self-proclaimed Tsar, Grand Duke Kyril, who now lived in exile in northern France with his wife, Victoria's cousin Victoria Melita, former Grand Duchess of Hesse.

In the final paragraph of her memoirs, Victoria wrote that she felt a fresh life had been opened to her. They would live a simple, quiet life, 'devoting a great deal of our time to work, and later travelling abroad and visiting friends'.[4] Zoubkoff was naturally very contented with his sudden good fortune, and probably considered himself a lucky man. He had just acquired considerable wealth and status, and the promise of an easy life in which he would never want for anything. To suggest that he reciprocated the love of a widow more than twice his age is stretching the bounds of credulity, but he certainly recognised the strength of her passion for him. He would confide in friends and acquaintances, somewhat tastelessly, that she had been very enthusiastic and grateful, and that for a woman of sixty she was not a bad bargain.

Victoria entrusted her business affairs to Zoubkoff without reservation, and he wasted no time in spending his newly acquired fortune. Within a month or so after their wedding, he had returned to his old haunts and gambling habits in the casinos and nightclubs of Berlin. Because he was the former Kaiser's brother-in-law, he was given unlimited credit at first, a facility of which he made full use.

In February 1928, Zoubkoff was contacted by one of his associates, a Mr Solski, who was making plans to fly across the Atlantic in an aeroplane. Air travel was still a novelty, and the scheme was to take a German plane to Ireland, then cross the ocean to Newfoundland and then to the United States. All Solski needed was the initial finance of 50,000 marks (£2,500). When Zoubkoff put the scheme to Victoria, she was initially very enthusiastic, but could not provide more than a small part of the initial funds. She suggested that they approach a banker in Berlin for the remainder. They accordingly sent letters out and received a few interested replies, asking Her Imperial Highness and her husband to visit them and discuss the proposal. At least one of them suggested that the flight could partly be funded by mortgaging the Schaumburg Palace, an idea to which Victoria apparently made no objection at first.

Confident that the venture would be a tremendous success that would garner him international renown, Zoubkoff announced his plans to the press. He and Solski would take it in turns to pilot the aeroplane, and his wife would be the first passenger from Germany to cross the Atlantic by air. An agreement was drafted and signed by all three at the office of a lawyer in Berlin, according to which Herr and Frau Zoubkoff would be the main beneficiaries of any revenue generated by the story of the flight, its sale to the press, and any other resulting income. With this in mind, Zoubkoff booked a suite at the Hotel Adlon, Berlin, to hold a press conference. He was in his element and answered all the questions, while Victoria was uncomfortable with the attention. Newspapers in Europe and the United States still reported eagerly on anything to do with the couple, some with more accuracy than others: three months after the wedding, one provincial American journal told its readers that the princess's romance had ended, as her husband had suffered a nervous breakdown and was confined in an asylum.[7]

Uneasiness with publicity did not, however, prevent Victoria from eagerly anticipating the event. When Zoubkoff took her and Solski to meet the first of the bankers on their list, they were told that his bank would help to meet the costs of the transatlantic flight, but in return would require a mortgage on the palace and 25 per cent of all income as security for the project. Victoria was reluctant to commit herself at once, and they were given a few days to discuss the proposal, prior to a second meeting. By then, Zoubkoff claimed that he had received a generous offer from a newspaper for a series of articles on the flight; she was persuaded that a mortgage would not be quite so great a risk as she had initially believed.

Within days of committing to a loan to this effect, Victoria began to have second thoughts about the wisdom of this investment, if it could be considered thus. Since the wedding, she had been only too happy to adjust herself to her husband's extravagant lifestyle; the couple dined at fine restaurants and frequented nightclubs and cabarets, accumulating bills for vodka and champagne. However, it was soon to turn very sour. At around this time Zoubkoff instigated a brawl with the staff at a Berlin restaurant which prompted the arrival of the police. He was summoned to court in Berlin, and on 24 February appeared for a cross-examination, during which it became apparent that he did not possess a valid permit to live in the city. He was fined 500 marks (£25), and once a previous fine of 100 marks for a similar offence was disclosed, was warned that he would probably be expelled from Germany.[5]

Victoria was thoroughly shaken by this public display of behaviour. By this time she had also been shown a bank statement which revealed the full extent of Zoubkoff's profligate spending. Her bankers warned her that his debts—in other words, their shared debts—were mounting rapidly, and that their financial resources were near exhausted. Since the wedding, Victoria's allowance from the Schaumburg-Lippe family had been discontinued and her estrangement from most of her Hohenzollern relations meant that she could expect no support from them. It equally transpired that Zoubkoff stole and sold the princess's jewellery for ready cash when more credit was denied him. He was openly unfaithful, and the German press fervently tracked his association with a variety of chorus girls, actresses, and prostitutes during his gambling trips to Paris, Monte Carlo, and Wiesbaden. In spite of Victoria's distaste for confrontation and the endurance of her affection, the veil had been lifted.

Unsurprisingly, the banker who had offered to help finance their expedition withdrew from the project and refused to have any further dealings with Zoubkoff or his scheme. The princess, he said, would have to finance the flight herself. The idea of a flight across the Atlantic, and of a newspaper offering generous sums for the exclusive rights to their story, was rapidly turning into fantasy.

The final break between Victoria and her new husband came when he tried to persuade her to agree to a Hollywood film to be made of their 'romance', for which they would travel to the United States and play themselves. Their fee would be $150,000 plus expenses, a sum which would clear their accrued debts in a single stroke. For the princess, the suggestion was inconceivable and represented the final straw.

This was probably the last occasion on which they saw each other. Zoubkoff's debts are now estimated to have been of around 600,000 marks; he was warned that the Ministry of the Interior in Berlin would shortly be issuing him with an expulsion order. He would be required to permanently leave Germany by the nearest border with no possibility of returning, and was only given advanced notice out of consideration for his wife. He decided to become a resident of Luxembourg—being virtually stateless, this was one of the only options open to him. Had his offence solely been a passport and visa violation, the authorities might have been more accommodating, but his unremitting misconduct, compounded by the notoriety of his marriage, made certain his expulsion from national frontiers. There are also grounds for suspecting that either the former Crown Prince Wilhelm (who still lived in the country) or the exiled Kaiser himself may have asked the authorities to intercede. He thereafter attempted to visit his wife in Germany several times, but each request for permission to enter Germany was rejected.

In April 1928, Zoubkoff was arrested at Arlon, near the Luxembourg frontier, in connection with irregularities in his passport. Some have suggested that he repeatedly wrote to the former Kaiser, asking for funds to help 'poor Vicky', but that his letters were ignored. If the accounts of relatives on his mother's side are to be believed, it was Victoria who came to visit him in Luxembourg and in other countries.[6] The veracity of this version of events remains open to interpretation; given that contact between them had been severed under the close watch of Victoria's remaining entourage, it seems unlikely that they met each other again.

From around this time onwards, Victoria's health began to fail. She took to her bed under the strain of impending financial catastrophe and the end of her marriage, suffering from depression and heart trouble. Her devoted maid Clara Franz remained with her at the Schaumburg Palace to nurse her, but this was her only consolation.

Though she may have been justified in adopting a less conciliatory stance, the former Queen Sophie of Greece was bore no lasting grudge against England at the downfall and premature death of her husband. 'I am so homesick and dying to see dear England again,' she wrote from Florence to King George V, asking to sojourn there for a while after sending Princess Katherine to school for the summer term at Broadstairs.

> I have absolutely nothing to do with politics ... so I hope I can give no offence by living quietly—and out of the world in a small place if my means permit. I am too old and sad and tired to go out in society. Journeys are so expensive and life in England especially so, I could only afford a very simple lodging.[8]

From a distance she followed events in the lives of her cousins at Windsor with unfailing interest. When King George V recovered from a serious illness during the winter of 1928-29—which some had feared could prove fatal—Sophie sent him a message to express her delight. It was 'the greatest joy', she said, to see his picture in the papers again. She doubtless recognised the weightier role played by the French administration than that of the British in the Allies' campaign against her country during the war. While Sophie felt antipathy for the French Republic, England, her second childhood home, was still the country of her cousin King George.

Sophie also showed a willingness to forgive past injuries when, on the occasion of her eldest brother's seventieth birthday in January 1929, she made a special journey to Doorn to join the family celebration. The same may not be said for her brother who, although somewhat mellowed since his abdication ten years ago, greeted her with polite formality. He afterwards wrote with some excitement to an American friend, the journalist Poultney Bigelow, of how much he had enjoyed being surrounded by his children and grandchildren of all ages, no less than nineteen altogether, and then, as an afterthought, also by his sisters.

Among the assembled was Margaret, with whom the Kaiser had never truly fallen out with. Certainly, he had once regarded Margaret contemptuously, alongside Victoria and Sophie, as part of 'the English colony' fostered by their Anglophile mother, but the youngest sister was the only one who had never incurred his wrath. For her own part, Margaret had been angered by his treatment of their mother during her widowhood, and by his and the Empress's high-handed attitude towards Sophie over her change of religion; for many years she and her husband had kept their distance. And yet, Wilhelm had admired the fortitude with which she and her husband had faced the loss of their two eldest sons in the war; and for Margaret, the Empress's death had removed a barrier and enabled her to show her brother increasing sympathy in his loneliness and exile. Regular contact between brother and sister had thus been established once more, and although they were living in different countries, their relationship became closer over the years.[9] The situation between the Kaiser and his younger brother, whom he had never taken seriously, had likewise not been easy, and he had never got on well with his sons either. In many ways, Margaret and Friedrich Karl were the only members of the family from his generation that he had left. As he could not visit her in Germany, she and Friedrich Karl came to see him at Doorn from time to time, and it was something for which he remained grateful.

A similar friendship did not exist between the Kaiser and his two other sisters. The disgraced Victoria, who had so tarnished the family name, did not feature on the birthday guest list. In the brief conversation he had with Sophie, he never once made any reference to her past sorrows, or enquired about any of her future plans. They spoke like two strangers meeting for the first time; she returned to Frankfurt feeling hurt and embittered. They would never see each other again.

In January 1929, a group of clerks arrived at Schaumburg Palace to make a full inventory of what remained and could be offered for sale. Zoubkoff's creditors still needed to be paid and they were unlikely to leave Victoria alone. She was confined to bed by her illness most of the time, and so was allowed to remain in residence in two rooms on the first floor of the palace. With the onset of better weather in March, and after several weeks of rest, she slowly regained her strength.

That summer, *My Memoirs* by Princess Victoria of Prussia was published. The English edition, priced at twenty-one shillings, was reviewed in June by *The Times*. The anonymous reviewer, who called it 'somewhat naive' and 'mostly personal and domestic', noted that the author 'describes herself as pro-English, and writes quite uncontroversially about the War and subsequent events'.[11] Those expecting revealing insights into her difficult relationships with several of her relatives were to be sorely disappointed. She dealt very briefly with the tale of her thwarted romance with Prince Alexander of Battenberg, and made no allusion to the fierce opposition to the match from her siblings and Hohenzollern grandparents. She commented that 'the marriage was definitely broken off by other people,' who had acted, uninvited, on her behalf; she did not enter into her own feelings, but conceded that her mother 'never forgot the part Bismarck had played and never forgave him'.[12] The imperial chancellor, not her relations, was to blame. A concise and very glowing character sketch of Kaiser Wilhelm at the start of the war alluded to 'his kindness of heart, his conscientiousness and his sincere piety', and how unbearable it had been 'to see the whole weight of the world's greatest misfortune put upon him, and to hear people trying to make him out a sort of blood-thirsty tyrant'. Those who knew him intimately, she added, would agree that 'to converse with him is really fascinating'.[13] She evaded any acknowledgement of the tensions that had existed between Kaiser Wilhelm and King George during the war, remarking that a state visit paid by the Kaiser and Empress to England in November 1907 'seemed to have been very useful in making stronger the bonds that existed between uncle and nephew'.[14] Equally benevolent were her recollections of Charlotte, her gossip-loving sister; she noted, somewhat unconvincingly, that Charlotte 'had been popular all her life; and to the end was kind and generous, hard-working and sympathetic towards all'.[15]

By the time it was published and complimentary copies were sent to her in Bonn, Victoria had lost interest and the parcel was left unopened. It is likely that any royalties arrived too late.

Another, more important contribution to family history was published in the autumn of 1928, comprising several hundred letters written by the Empress Frederick to Queen Victoria throughout her married life and widowhood. A few months before her death, Queen Victoria personally entrusted these to her godson Sir Frederick Ponsonby, who was also private secretary to King Edward VII and King George V consecutively. In his possession, they were kept safe and unread in England for over a quarter of a century. Distorted portrayals of the Empress—as a callous mother, or power-crazed meddler in German affairs—in works such as Emil Ludwig's 1926 biography of Kaiser Wilhelm II progressively incensed Ponsonby, and eventually provoked him to retaliate. He first consulted a hesitant King George on the matter and was advised to do what he thought fit; he then selected for publication extracts from the letters and constructed a biography around them.

The resulting book, *Letters of the Empress Frederick*, caused a sensation upon its appearance in October 1928. Some of the British royal family were dismayed by the controversy, but others were very supportive. The Empress's surviving siblings were divided, with Beatrice calling it 'dreadful' upon reading extracts in the newspapers, while the Duke of Connaught and Duchess of Argyll pronounced that Ponsonby had done the right thing.

Queen Sophie and Margaret, who were firmly convinced that their mother had entrusted Ponsonby with the letters in order that he publish them when he felt the time was right, were particularly grateful to him for having done her memory justice. When he sent them copies of the book, they thanked him for carrying out her wishes; the Landgravine signed her letter, 'Yours sincerely and gratefully, Margaret'.[16] She wrote to Lady Corkran:

> You can imagine what it means to me to read my beloved mother's letters & to go through all those times again.... Sir F. wrote me a beautiful letter explaining his reasons for publishing the book, & I quite understand. From his point of view he was quite right to do so, but here people of course take a different view. I believe the Emperor is very put out & upset about it.[17]

As he had not been consulted beforehand, the former Kaiser was furious and threatened to sue for breach of copyright, claiming the letters were his. At length and upon legal consultation, he accepted that his case was somewhat weak, and that pursuing the matter would further harm his reputation. As a compromise, he purchased the rights to the German edition on condition that he write its preface. He did so, and in it referred to his mother's sensitivity and to how she 'saw want of sympathy and coolness when there was only a helpless silence'; he concluded that the reader ought not to believe everything she wrote.[18] His daughter, Victoria Louise, had a similarly scathing reaction to the appearance of the book, noting in her memoirs that it not only 'revealed' to the public the attitude of the Kaiser towards his mother, but it also 'helped its author [or more correctly editor] out of his financial straits, [and] illustrated how it apparently gave him authority to publish other people's letters'.[19]

Victoria, or Frau Zoubkoff as the newspapers now referred to her, would undoubtedly have shared her sisters' feelings on the subject, but she voiced no reaction. Her silence on the matter perhaps reflected its trivial significance in light of ordeals which the disenchanted, ailing woman was herself facing at the time. In September 1929, the final disgrace came: in order to defray some of her debts, the courts ruled that the remaining contents of her palace be sold at public auction, and that she be evicted from the estate. In her poor condition and after decades spent at Schaumburg Palace, eviction proved to be the final blow.[20]

The auction was held in Bonn on 15 October. Catalogues were sold in advance and representatives of major art dealers in London were despatched; interest in heirlooms from the estate of Queen Victoria bequeathed to the Empress Frederick, and in turn to the latter's second daughter, caught on. Although Kaiser Wilhelm did not immediately show the matter any attention, he contacted the chief auctioneer in due course to suggest that such items be offered to the British royal family. Nobody apparently acted on this advice, though one would assume that he would at least have received some form of reply. There was speculation that either he or King George V might intervene and that one, if not both, would send a delegation to purchase everything, but neither did.

The opening bids suggested that the value or importance of the goods had been seriously overestimated. Moreover, given the devaluation of the German mark in the 1920s, and the glut of royal merchandise saturating the market in post-revolutionary Europe, this was probably the worst possible time to sell with any expectation of a fair return. The bidding was reported to be 'spiritless', and several items were sold at strangely low prices. First to go under the hammer were the contents of a valuable silver chamber, much of which was the work of ancient London silversmiths. A large oval Baroque tureen with a lid of worked silver and artistic decoration, made in 1750 and consisting of 113 ounces of silver, went to a Swiss bidder for 6,000 marks (£300). Another similar tureen, which had been valued at 20,000 marks (£1,000), fetched only 3,200 marks (£160). Saddest of all was the offer of a silver bust of Kaiser Friedrich, for which no bids were made. After the opening price was reduced by one-half, it was purchased by an English dealer for 110 marks (£5 10s). Because the bust contained 55 ounces of silver, this price was below the actual market value of the metal. Rather more interest was shown in the afternoon, when various small objects were bought by the public at more realistic prices. Nevertheless, the overall results of the sale proved disappointing. The princess's debts amounted to 900,000 marks (£45,000), and it was estimated that the proceeds would only be enough to cover about one third of this sum.

After the auction, an American newspaper reported that the princess was found by one of the servants outside in the garden, clutching the trunk of one of her trees. She was said to be looking dazed. It is possible that she had set her hopes on the chance that one of her relatives would purchase several items, or that they would send out an injunction to prevent the sale from going ahead.

Victoria's maid, Clara, was able to find her a room in the suburb of Mehlem, furnished with a bed, a couple of armchairs, and a worn carpet but little else. It was a pitiful contrast to the palace that she had known and loved for so many years. Wearily, she instructed her solicitor to begin divorce proceedings against the man who had only been her husband in name. But nothing really mattered any more, and she was gradually losing interest in life. She was unable to pay Clara a proper wage, and would not hear of her last friend and devotee working without payment. Although she was sent away, Clara secretly rented a room in the neighbourhood to keep an eye on her mistress.

Ostracised by most of her family and now completely alone, Victoria spent her time in bed, bitterly depressed, sobbing for hours on end and crying herself to sleep. A neglected cold turned into pneumonia, and on 6 November 1929, a doctor forced his way into her room, where he found her in a critical condition with a high fever. With his assistance she was admitted to St Francis's Hospital in Bonn. Members of her family were alerted that the end could be near. Heinrich had died aged sixty-six in April 1929 from pneumonia and bronchitis, which made the former Kaiser Victoria's only surviving brother. Deeply concerned, he telephoned the hospital twice a day for news of her condition. Margaret, who had been more sympathetic to her plight than the rest of the family, made a special journey to Bonn, but was not allowed in to see her.

It was observed that there was no similar response from the former Queen of Greece. Though Victoria and Sophie had been close in childhood, there is some indication that Sophie agreed with their brother about the shame brought on the family by her sister's disastrous second marriage. On the other hand, Sophie may have been just as concerned as her siblings, but simply preoccupied with her own health, which at the time was also beginning to fail.

In any case, Victoria lost the will to fight her illness, and her condition deteriorated sharply. An attack of influenza developed into acute inflammation of the lungs, and on 13 November 1929, a week after being admitted to hospital, she died, aged of sixty-three. It was rumoured that she had even taken her own life in despair, or tried to drown herself. Almost exactly two years earlier, she had entered, for the second time, into a marriage which she believed would transform her life. She was proven right, and few princesses had known a more pathetic end. Yet in death, her last wishes were faithfully respected; the next day, Victoria's body was taken to Friedrichshof. The same day, Zoubkoff made his way to Bonn having learned of her death, but was arrested for having illegally entered Germany. On 16 November, she was laid to rest in the chapel beside the bodies of her nephews Max and Friedrich Wilhelm of Hesse-Cassel. Three members of her family were present—the ever-supportive Margaret, Heinrich's widow Irene, and Prince Adalbert of Prussia, representing his father in Doorn.

Zoubkoff survived his wife by six years. He remained in Luxembourg, and there were stories of his enduringly peripatetic career in the grand duchy. One suggests that he coaxed a cabaret owner into employing him as a Russian folksinger and advertised himself as 'Alexander Zoubkoff, who married the Kaiser's sister'. Another relates that he sought work as a waiter in a cafe, advising the owner that it would be good for business to publicise that customers would be served by the Kaiser's brother-in-law.[21] Wilhelm allegedly tried to take the proprietor to court in an attempt to have the notice on the street to this effect removed, but in vain.

Zoubkoff remained a widower, having experienced only a few

incongruous months of married life. Indulgence in drink and drugs took their toll, and in January 1936 it was reported in the papers that he had died in Luxembourg 'in reduced circumstances'.[22] On the day of his death, a woman calling herself Marie Zoubkoff claiming to be his mother went to the authorities and asked for the death certificate of her son Alexander. According to other sources, however, his mother had died in 1927. Separating fact from fiction in the Zoubkoff family narrative has historically been an arduous task.

By the end of the 1920s, one of the Empress Frederick's *Kleeblatt* had died, and another did not have long to live. Queen Sophie had admitted to not feeling quite herself for some time, complaining of nerves, painful acidity, and loss of appetite. A visit to a French specialist, and later to a clinic in Frankfurt, resulted in a temporary improvement in her health, but this was not to be sustained.

She continued to travel widely and keep in touch with members of her family. Her sister-in-law, Alice, with whom her relations had never been easy, had suffered a nervous breakdown and was diagnosed with paranoid schizophrenia. In August 1930, Queen Sophie paid her a visit at the sanatorium in Kreuzlingen, Switzerland, where she was being treated, but sadly deduced that coherent conversation with her was no longer conceivable. On the day of Sophie's visit, Alice's youngest daughter, another Sophie, also came to see her mother and found her spirits improved. It might then be construed that time had eroded some of the ill-feeling that there had been between Sophie and her sister-in-law.

In the spring of 1931, Sophie visited Munich and then spent several enjoyable weeks in England. Conversely, this was not a happy time for one of the *Kleeblatt*'s cousins, Queen Victoria Eugenie of Spain, or her husband, King Alfonso XIII, who had gone into exile. Sophie in particular could relate to the circumstances of their exile, in view of their resemblance to the events of 1917. To Margaret also, their cousin's news was another reminder of the precariousness of sovereigns in the twentieth century. 'The events in Spain were indeed terrible,' Margaret wrote to Lady Corkran. 'What a shame to treat the King like that, who had been so excellent in every way. That poor country will probably go to rack and ruin now.'[23]

After arriving in England in July with her younger daughters Irene and Katherine and her son Paul, Sophie stayed with two old friends, Colonel and Mrs James Horlick, and went to visit her daughter-in-law Aspasia and her granddaughter Alexandra. In the middle of the month, she called upon King George V and Queen Mary at Buckingham Palace. In August, she and her daughters made charitable visits to Middlesex Hospital, the Hospital for Sick Children on Great Ormond Street, and upon invitation, the British College of Nurses at Portland Place, where Sophie was received by the President and members of the Council. It was a busy programme, but she enjoyed being active, and to all outward appearances she seemed to have made a good recovery from an earlier bout of ill-health. However, by the time she arrived in Venice in September, she was complaining of feeling ill and uncomfortable with the heat.

In November, Sophie was admitted to hospital at Frankfurt 'for an internal complaint from which she has long since suffered'; she was diagnosed with cancer. Her children and sister were told that the disease was at an advanced, inoperable stage and that she only had a few weeks to live. Although Sophie was never informed of this, it may well have crossed her mind that she was suffering from the affliction that had claimed the lives of both her parents at a similar age. She was too ill to be moved back to Florence, and the family gathered around her hospital bed. Among her visitors were her daughter-in-law Aspasia Manos, and her eleven-year-old granddaughter Alexandra. She had a small Christmas tree beside her bed, and asked the girl to light the candles for her. It was the last time they ever saw each other.[24]

As she watched Sophie grow gradually weaker, Margaret observed that she tried to remain cheerful, despite her illness:

> she cannot understand why she is so weak, a sign that it has been possible to keep the truth from her.... It is difficult to find the right nourishment as all food disgusts her, & she often suffers from sickness.[25]

She was given regular injections and spent much of the time sleeping, unable to do anything else. Over Christmas, she seemed to recover to a degree, but in the first week of the New Year 1932, she suffered a relapse. 'It is all so cruel,' Margaret wrote on 6 January. 'She seemed so depressed this evening & wonders why she does not get better.'[26] The family, if not she herself, knew by now that it would only be a matter of time; she died peacefully one week later.

Her body was taken to lie in state in the great hall at Friedrichshof, and a small family funeral service was held at Kronberg three days later. It was then taken to Florence, where another funeral was held on 21 January at the Russian Orthodox Church, at which the King and Queen were represented by Vivian Bosanquet, British Consul-General at Frankfurt. She was then laid to rest in the crypt beside the remains of King Constantine and Queen Olga. The Florentine villa she had loved was bought by her daughter Helen, renamed the Villa Sparta, and became a family home for her exiled sons and daughters.

Margaret was devastated by the death, and six weeks later wrote to Lady Corkran that it was a loss she would never overcome:

Sometimes I try hard not to think, but it is a useless struggle. She is always present wherever I am or whatever I do, as she always was, ever since I exist[ed]. Those terrible two months & all that followed afterwards still haunt me.[27]

Sophie's second daughter Irene also felt 'stunned' by her mother's passing. She wrote to a friend in March, saying:

Having lost both our beloved parents life doesn't seem worth living any more & one misses them every day more.... The only consolation is that at least they are happier on the other side without all the trials & difficulties of this hard life.[28]

In spite of the rifts in their relationship, the former Kaiser was affected by the death of his sister. His daughter the Duchess of Brunswick noted that his seventy-third birthday later that month was the quietest he had ever spent, for reasons besides his own sickness. After she had attended the funeral at Kronberg, the Duchess reported to him in detail, and spoke of her meeting with their Greek relatives. Wilhelm agreed with her that they had 'all gone through a great deal'.[29]

Some of the tributes paid to Sophie in the press were guarded, and a few were less than sympathetic. As Sir Rennell Rodd, a Unionist MP and former British ambassador to Italy, pointed out in a short appreciation in *The Times*, some of the obituary notices gave evidence of 'a considerable prejudice' against her and King Constantine dating back to the First World War. While he did not wish to examine or judge the accuracy of rumours about the couple, he felt it only right to revere the memory of a woman who was a true daughter of a remarkable mother. He depicted her as 'less brilliantly gifted perhaps and less combative in spirit, but endowed with a similar charm and a natural sweetness of disposition, a kind friend and a most devoted mother', and paid tribute to her spending the last few years of 'a broken life' in dignity, and to her 'commendable reserve as an exile ... under circumstances pathetically different from those she had seemed entitled to anticipate'.[30]

Had Queen Sophie lived for another four years, she would have witnessed the restoration of Greece to a kingdom once more in November 1935, and her eldest son George, now divorced from his cousin Elisabetha, claim the throne. This reversal of royal fortune was some comfort to Margaret, though it made her 'so sad to think of all my darling sister & her husband were made to suffer'.[31] The palace at Tatoi returned to the property of the Greek royal family, and King George and Queen Olga's remains finally interred in the royal burial ground.

'The fingers of the acquisitive' 1932–54

Margaret, Landgrave of Hesse-Cassel, the last remaining of the four daughters of Kaiser and Empress Frederick, would live through the troubled 1930s and another world war. She survived the Second World War, and afterwards came to know the world in its new order, a harsh contrast from the life that she and her family had known. According to the poet Siegfried Sassoon, who had enjoyed an intimate relationship with Margaret's son Philipp for some years prior to the latter's marriage, Philipp had harboured a 'not unnatural bitterness about the downfall of his family prestige.' Sassoon wrote that he 'deeply regrets the disappearance of the environment in which he was brought up'.[1] It was a view shared to some extent by his parents and surviving brothers. Impressed by Fascism while on a visit to Italy, Philipp joined the Nazi party in October 1930, leading the way for the rest of the Hesse-Cassel family. Through his membership of the party he became friends with Hermann Goering, the future head of the German *Luftwaffe*. Philipp rose to become a major figure in the party, a member of the Reichstag, and later governor of Hesse-Nassau. As a son-in-law of King Victor Emmanuel of Italy, he acted as an important go-between for Adolf Hitler and Benito Mussolini.

In November 1930, his brother Christoph married Sophie of Greece and Denmark at Friedrichshof, and among the youngest of the family guests was the bride's nine-year-old brother Philip, the future Duke of Edinburgh. In 1931, Christoph joined the Nazi party, and was followed by Richard and Wolfgang a year later.

Margaret was one of many to perceive promising signs in the new German Chancellor. In May 1932, she complained that there was not the slightest chance of paying another visit to 'dear old England', although she desperately longed to see the country again.

They have made travelling almost impossible over here, as we are not allowed to step more than 200m out of this country. We have been through every sort of excitement with all the different elections, wh[ich] certainly mean a step forward, but have not managed to change our impossible government. However, we feel sure that things cannot go on much longer as they are now. Hitler's movement is our great hope. He is a wonderful man, & I regret to see that people in England have no idea of his personality or what his aim is. If Bolshevism has become less dangerous over here it is only owing to him. He is the only man who can save us from Communism & Socialism, wh[ich] have brought us to the state we are in now.[2]

Like her eldest brother, and in stark contrast to their parents, she shared the anti-Semitism prevalent among some sections of German society. 'So sad for me to see England against us once more, & the Jewish influence so evident,' she wrote nearly a year later. 'Those horrible lies that have been spread are their revenge. Where has a revolution taken place without bloodshed, & in such a peaceful & orderly way as this one?'[3] Keen to register their support and play their part in a glorious future, Margaret and Friedrich Karl also became members of the Nazi party in 1938.

Interestingly, and despite his anti-Jewish prejudices, Margaret's brother was less enthusiastic, and only one of the former Kaiser's sons, August Wilhelm, ever became a member. Nevertheless, the former Kaiser was on good terms with some leading members of the party, particularly Goering, who visited him in Doorn in 1931 and 1932. The Nazi government provided him, the former Crown Prince, and the other Prussian princes, with a substantial annual allowance from the Prussian state, on condition that they make no public criticism of the party or Hitler. But the former Kaiser showed inconsistency in his position, and was constantly alternating between praise and dismissal of Hitler.[4] On some occasions, he would rail against the Jewish race—in 1929 he wrote to a friend saying that that Jews and mosquitoes were 'a nuisance that humanity must get rid of in some way or other' (he believed gas to be the best solution).[5] At other times he would deplore Hitler's treatment of them, and once admitted to being ashamed to be German.[6] In private, he was horrified by the escalation of anti-Semitic vandalism and attacks that led to *Kristallnacht*, and expressed his disgust at such 'pure bolshevism!' to Queen Mary in England.[7] Yet, and at the same time, he refrained from taking a public stand on these developments, and it was not long before he reverted to making furiously anti-Semitic remarks in his correspondence.

Margaret persisted in hoping that, one day, her brother or, failing him, another member of the family might be restored to their former position.

Only a few years after the Kaiser's abdication, she had been quoted by his adjutant, Sigurd von Ilsemann, as having wished 'with all her heart for a return of the Kaiser to the throne'.[8] The chances of such an event were negligible, even if he had shown enthusiasm for resuming a public function, or indeed the sovereignty. In 1933, the American and French ambassadors discussed President Hindenburg's plans to bring about a monarchical restoration on the German throne, but they were averse to selecting a Hohenzollern. Neither the seventy-six-year-old former Kaiser nor his idle and dissolute eldest son were judged suitable candidates. The only plausible name raised was that of Ernst, Duke of Hesse and the Rhine. Significantly, the personable Ernst was one of a diminishing minority of German royals who had made no serious adversaries and had been on uninterruptedly good terms with his English cousin King George V. The latter wrote to him in 1935, a few months before his death, that 'that horrible and unnecessary war [the First World War] has made no difference in my feelings for you'.[9]

The death of King George in January 1936, and abdication of King Edward VIII within less than a year of succeeding to it, shocked and 'upset' Margaret. 'There must be more reasons than we know, otherwise it is inconceivable,' she wrote to Lady Corkran, a week after the abdication. 'He [Edward VIII] seemed so promising, so many good qualities, such a sound judgment, & then this! Perhaps all is for the best.'[10] She took a similar interest in the new King, and six months later thanked Lady Corkran for a letter and book about the coronation at Westminster Abbey. Margaret followed the service on the radio, which evoked memories of a similar ceremony held for the King's father a quarter of a century earlier. She appreciated how exhausting the new monarch and his consort may have found the proceedings: 'The poor King & Queen must be wanting a rest badly.'[11]

Unsurprisingly, Margaret looked with increasing alarm on the state of Europe. Hostility towards Germany distressed her. 'The vile propaganda campaign against us almost reminds us of the year 14!' she noted, just a few days before the coronation. 'It is too wicked, & alas people are always foolish enough to believe lies.'[12] For a while, she shared in the general optimism that the Munich agreement of 30 September 1938, permitting the German annexation of Sudetenland, had brought Neville Chamberlain's 'peace in our time'. She followed the progress of events with apprehension and excitement, and assured Lady Corkran that the annexation augured well for the future:

One can hope and pray that last night's conference will mean a turning point in history, that truth & justice will gain the upper hand & the

vile intrigues & misunderstandings of the last thirty years no longer
be allowed to cause such danger. Thank God that men of courage &
common sense have at last come forward in other countries too.
Certainly, our beloved Führer & Mussolini stand on a very high pinnacle,
& Mr C has been much admired & appreciated here too. We spend most
of our time at the wireless as you can imagine.[13]

Yet within a few months, it became increasingly evident that Europe
would soon be engulfed in a conflict no less terrible than the previous one.
Once again, Margaret was pained at Europe's, and particularly England's,
image of Germany, yet she did not waiver in her patriotic conviction. In
April 1939, she gave vent to her fears in another letter to Lady Corkran:

> Oh dear, oh dear, may enlightenment come before it is too late. I always
> told you there was so much ill-feeling towards this country in leading
> quarters, & none at all here. The single object of weakening this country
> can only lead to disaster. Intrigues against us only make us stronger.
> Old antiquated ideas of balance of power & encirclement do not work
> anymore, the world is going new ways.[14]

Three months later, several members of royalty gathered at Florence
for the wedding of Sophie's daughter Irene to Prince Aimone, Duke of
Aosta and of Spoleto. Margaret's niece, the Duchess of Brunswick, made
use of the occasion to share with her aunt her owns fears that war was
fast approaching. Curiously, Margaret offered a more sanguine view of
the matter, arguing against the possibility that Hitler would deliberately
provoke confrontation. It was the Duchess's opinion that her aunt simply
could not bring herself to question the statesman in whom she has seen
such potential.[15] Within two months, war between Britain and Germany
broke out for the second time in twenty-five years.

On 28 May 1940, Friedrich Karl became ill and died, aged seventy-two.
He was succeeded as Landgrave of Hesse-Cassel and head of the family by
Philipp. As Friedrich Karl lay dying, news reached him of early German
victories, to which he responded with as robust a 'Heil Hitler!' salute as
he could muster. Hitler, in recognition of the Hesse-Cassels' unequivocal
support, sent a wreath of condolence to Margaret, who wrote back an
effusive letter of thanks. In it she referred to 'the ceaseless loyalty and
admiration' of her husband for the Führer 'as well as for the rise of the
Fatherland'. Not a day had passed, she assured him, when her husband did
not speak of Hitler, whom he 'followed until the very end the overpowering
events that he had long sensed were coming'. The letter ended with a clear
endorsement of Hitler's policies and objectives: 'may [God] crown you

with success in all the further great goals; that would be my own and my family's lasting wish, as well as that of my beloved husband.'[16]

On 12 September 1940, King George VI and Queen Elizabeth of Great Britain were standing at a window in Buckingham Palace when two bombs exploded in the courtyard outside in a plot to assassinate them. They realised afterwards that they were fortunate not to have been killed or at least maimed by flying glass. For some years, it was believed that this attempt had been planned or carried out, or both, by Margaret's son Christoph. It was said that he was intent on avenging the death of his brother Maximilian in the previous war, and that he 'had frequently been heard declaring how much he would like to bomb Buckingham Palace'.[17] Then again, his poor eyesight had prevented him from becoming a pilot, and he had been posted to Comiso in Italy; even if he did contribute to planning the assassination attempt, it seems very unlikely that he had any part in its execution. The accusation was firmly refuted by members of the British and German royal families, Christoph's brother-in-law, Philipp, not least among them.[18]

Two months later, bolstered by reports of military successes, Kaiser Wilhelm wrote with exhilaration to Margaret that the hand of God was 'creating a world & working miracles'. Recent feats in battle, he predicted, were the catalyst for Germany 'becoming the U.S. of Europe', and Europe 'a united German Continent'.[19] He did not live to see the tide turn against Germany: the following summer, on 4 June 1941, he died peacefully at his home in Doorn after a short illness, aged eighty-two. It was strange twist of fate that Wilhelm, who had briefly been given up for dead at his birth, should outlive both his parents and all but one of his siblings. Margaret travelled to Holland to join his widow, surviving children, and her widowed sister-in-law Irene at the funeral nine days later.

As the grand matriarch of the family, Margaret opened the doors of the big house at Friedrichshof to her remaining family during the war. Among those who found a ready welcome there was her nephew August Wilhelm, fourth son of the Kaiser.

As German victory in the conflict became less likely, the family's veneration of Hitler and the party leadership cooled. In April 1943, Philipp was summoned from Cassel by Hitler to meet him at his headquarters. Philipp thought he was going to be asked to undertake a mission to Italy, but instead he was placed under arrest without explanation. A month later, a decree concerning 'internationally Connected Men' declared that German princes would no longer be allowed to hold positions in the party, state, or armed forces. In July the Allies invaded Sicily, and Mussolini resigned and was arrested by King Victor Emmanuel. Philipp and his family were suspected of colluding in the Italian Premier's downfall. In September, he was accused of acting as an informant for the Italian royal family and was stripped of his party membership and dismissed from the *Luftwaffe*. He was sent to the Gestapo prison in Berlin, and then to a concentration camp at Flossenburg, where he was held in solitary confinement for nearly two years before being transferred to Dachau. His family were not informed of his whereabouts. His wife Mafalda, whom Hitler was convinced was working against the German war effort and whom he labelled the 'blackest carrion in the Italian royal house' was also arrested and sent to the Buchenwald camp, where she was housed next to an armaments factory. It was rumoured, but never substantiated, that she was forced into prostitution during the last months of her life. During an air raid that summer, she suffered serious injuries to her arm, and after two days the doctors concluded that they would have to amputate it. She was already suffering from heart trouble, and during the operation she lost copious amounts of blood. She never regained consciousness and died on 27 August 1943.

Another of the Hesse-Cassel princes now also fell under the scrutiny of the German high command. Christoph had joined the *Luftwaffe*, and probably would have met the same fate as his brother had he not died in a plane crash on 7 October 1943. He had been flying a fighter plane from Rome to Mannheim, which ploughed into the Apennine mountains near Forli in Italy. The wreckage and bodies of Christoph and his pilot were found two days later. The crash was ascribed to human error and thick fog, although speculation that a bomb had been planted aboard the aircraft held some sway. His mother-in-law Victoria, Marchioness of Milford Haven, was full of sympathy for his mother: 'this is the 3rd son she has lost in war, the two eldest in the last one & now her favourite in this one.'[20] Christoph's widow Sophie left Cassel and moved to Friedrichshof, where she gave birth to their fifth child, Clarissa, the following February. Further misfortune befell the family in 1944, when Wolfgang's wife Marie was killed in an air raid on Frankfurt by the American Air Force on 29 January. The only consolation was that she had no children to leave motherless.

Friedrichshof was unscathed by air raids, but Rupenheim, the family seat near Frankfurt, was left a gutted, black ruin. The family was sufficiently unnerved to take all possible precautions. They reclaimed the family jewels from the vaults of the Reichsbank in Frankfurt, including a number of items owned by Prince August Wilhelm. They made a full inventory, wrapped them individually in brown paper packages, with lists of the contents, and the names and addresses of the owners, and buried them in a zinc-lined chest constructed specially for the purpose, which was then taken to the Friedrichshof cellar and buried in a hole concealed by an expert stonemason. The best of their collections of furniture, paintings and tapestries were put into storage; the silverware was locked in a special vault; and the rare and valuable wines, over 1,600 bottles, were concealed behind a false wall. Some local businesses also stored some of their stock at the house.

In the spring of 1945, American troops arrived at Kronberg and a group of officers visited Friedrichshof. When Sophie, who was playing in the garden with her baby Clarissa, came to the gates to ask them what they wanted, they told her that the army required accommodation for about 300 men and a hundred vehicles. The estate administrator, Heinrich Lange, explained to the men that the house only had one bathroom. They left, but later returned and arrested August Wilhelm. They requisitioned the castle, Margaret's cottage in the grounds, and all neighbouring buildings in the park.

The Landgravine, Sophie, and nine grandchildren (Philipp and Mafalda's four children and Christoph and Sophie's five) were given four hours' notice to leave, and were only allowed to take food, clothing, and bed linen with them. As they were packing their possessions onto a cart, Margaret's grandson Moritz ran back into the house to remove one of their most valuable items, a silver mirror that had once belonged to Marie Antoinette. He wrapped it in a blanket and hid it inside the belongings of his aunt Sophie.

The Landgravine, who had been unwell and under severe stress for some time, was ill in bed at the time with double pneumonia and protested that she was not fit enough to be moved. One of the sergeants was indifferent, and snapped that if 'the old girl' did not come down at once, he would go up to her room and shoot her.[21] After some persuasion she bowed to the inevitable, and as a temporary measure she stayed in various houses nearby, sometimes for only one night at a time, before she found somewhere more permanent in a house just beyond the grounds of the estate. Sophie appealed to an American colonel to allow her ailing mother-in-law some space in one of her properties. She was then allowed to occupy two rooms in one of the houses on the estate. Margaret herself had grown exhausted, so Sophie assumed the matriarchal role.

The family had to split up, desperate to find refuge with anybody who would give them shelter. The day after the army requisitioned Friedrichshof, Philipp's second son Heinrich was resting in the house of his piano teacher when he heard a report of his mother Mafalda's death the previous summer on the radio. Until then, she had merely been presumed missing. In tears, he ran to the house where his aunt Sophie was staying.

She insisted at first that the story was American propaganda, but soon learned otherwise.

From England, matters were being viewed with alarm. In spite of relief at the unconditional surrender of Germany and cessation of hostilities a week after Hitler's suicide on 30 April, the Landgravine's home was still the repository of vitally important collections of royal papers. These were believed to include documents relating to the Duke (former King Edward VIII) and Duchess of Windsor, who had been suspected of sympathies for National Socialism ever since the Duke's abdication in 1936. An extensive archive of Queen Victoria's many letters to her eldest daughter may also have been at risk. In spite of wartime rifts, King George VI and the Landgravine were still second cousins—great-grandson and granddaughter of Queen Victoria—and he was gravely concerned at what he heard of the disarray at Friedrichshof, not least when a group of British Intelligence officers visited the house in July. Among them was Major Anthony Blunt, a fluent German-speaker with a background in espionage, who had recently been appointed Surveyor of the King's Pictures. He warned Sir Owen Morshead, the Royal Librarian, that the house and its contents were almost in pandemonium, and that irreplaceable papers of huge historical value were in danger of being 'exposed to the eyes of the inquisitive and the fingers of the acquisitive'.[22] Sir Alan Lascelles, the King's private secretary, was apprised of the situation by memo on 22 July.

On the King's instructions, and with the full permission of General Dwight D. Eisenhower, Supreme Commander of the Allied Forces in Europe, Blunt and Morshead flew to Frankfurt on 3 August to take precious letters from Friedrichshof to Windsor Castle. It is difficult to understate the extent to which the Landgravine, who had lost three of her six sons over the course of the two world wars, was supposed to have hated England. Her regular references in correspondence to 'dear old England' and her longing to return there suggest that this assessment was over-simplified, though she certainly emerged from the Second World War no longer the Anglophile that she had once been. Her daughter-in-law Sophie supported Blunt and Morshead when they asserted that the papers would be much safer with them, which was enough to persuade Margaret to agree to this arrangement as a temporary measure. She accordingly signed an agreement which gave them permission to take the letters.

British forces were required to observe strict regulations to try and prevent the looting of art, jewellery, and other personal and cultural possessions. These were, however, somewhat at variance with the guidelines given to the American forces, which allowed occupying forces to seize assets belonging to the Nazi party members. In addition, it was unclear whether the Landgravine of Hesse and her family, some of whom had previously been members, fell into this category at all. The princes, especially the Hohenzollerns, were still tainted by their association with the former Kaiser—demands for his trial as a war criminal were still within recent memory—and were regarded as undeserving of special treatment. In any case, the political distinctions between family members, and variations in treatment that could have been derived from these, were quickly rendered obsolete; the main house at Friedrichshof was unofficially turned into an American officers' club.

Officers and privates began to help themselves to some of the best furniture, moving it to Allied headquarters in Frankfurt, and vandalizing or breaking other pieces. Although rooms containing precious china, glass, and silverware, and the library with its priceless collection of books, were all ostensibly out of bounds, it remained easy for service personnel to help themselves to souvenirs. A few people were caught in the act, such as a couple of British officers trying to steal letters from Florence Nightingale, but for the most part, small thefts went undetected due to the difficulties of policing all passing military personnel. Family silver, items from china services, commemorative swords, medallions, and other objects gradually disappeared. Larger items, such as sculptures and paintings, among them a particularly fine canvas listed as 'School of Rubens', also gradually disappeared from the premises. The rare and valuable wines concealed behind a false wall were soon uncovered, and some papers are thought to have been burned. This violated standing orders, as documentation confirming the family's party membership—thus providing vital evidence in the event of a trial—may have been lost. The occupying military forces also helped themselves to the family peacocks that roamed the grounds and roasted them on a spit. This was seen as an act of flagrant cruelty, embittering the family further still. Interned and awaiting trial, Philipp at least was spared the harrowing sight of his family home being thus despoiled.

During the American Independence Day celebrations at Friedrichshof on 4 July 1945, clothing and toys which had belonged to the family were taken from the castle and given away to American military units for use as prizes at parties and bingo evenings. Prince Heinrich, Philipp's eighteen-year-old grandson, reported the loss of three items he had been given by his godfather, Kaiser Wilhelm II, including a gold cigarette holder, a gold bowl, and a gold pocket watch.

Yet the most serious theft was still to come. On 5 November, the manager of the club, Captain Kathleen Nash of the Women's Army Corps, and two other American officers, Major David Watson and Colonel Jack Durant (with whom Nash was romantically involved) entered the basement, supposedly looking for wine, and noticed a fresh patch of concrete in the wine cellar. They discovered the bricked-in enclosure, and with it the jewels which Wolfgang had carefully hidden under a stairway. At the same time they were also ostensibly looking for papers that might establish some connection between the Hesse-Cassel family and the Duke and Duchess of Windsor. If this was the case, what they came across may well have exceeded their wildest expectations. When the party chipped through the concrete, they discovered a zinc-lined box filled with small, neatly wrapped packets containing gold, silver, and jewels. The captain had the box taken to her room; she gave orders that she was not to be disturbed, and locked herself away for a day to examine the contents. She also sent for Heinrich Lange, and ordered him to hand over any further valuables, on the assurance that they would be kept safe and returned to the family at a later date. With great reluctance, he gave her the keys to the safe, but insisted on being given a receipt. He was also instructed to tell the Landgravine about what they had found. Although Margaret was concerned to learn that the Americans had come across them, she presumed that the military authorities would honour the letter of the law and eventually restore the jewels to their owners. Under the circumstances, she probably had no choice but to accept their word and trust them.[23]

But her trust—if that's what it was—was sorely misplaced. From the sequence of events that later transpired, it must be assumed that the three officers never had any intention of honouring their promises. Aware that attempting to smuggle the valuables back to the United States in their existing form would be asking for trouble, they removed the precious stones from their settings with the intention of concealing some and sending others away to sell later. They sold or pawned the gold and silver mountings. Watson spent a few weeks in Northern Ireland in November 1945 where he pawned a large amount of gold and gave a few smaller items to a former girlfriend. He also sent his parents a silver beaker which had been a Christmas gift to the Landgravine in 1927 from the King of Italy.

By this time, the Landgravine's daughter-in-law Sophie, Christoph's widow, was engaged to Prince Georg Wilhelm of Hanover, son of the Duchess of Brunswick. The wedding was to take place on 23 April 1946, and naturally she had planned to wear some of her jewellery on the day. Three months before the date of the ceremony she wrote to Captain Nash with a formal request for the return of her jewellery, silver, books, linen, and particular items of furniture as promised. Nash assured her that she would do all she could to expedite this, but she plainly had no intention of keeping to her agreement. A few days later she and Durant drove to Switzerland in an army staff car, secretly taking a large amount of gold and jewellery to sell. It was obvious to their prospective vendors in Berne that these were stolen items, and that any such purchases would be liable to immediate confiscation and criminal charges. Nash and Durant therefore had to use the Army post office system to send larger pieces, including a sterling silver pitcher, a thirty-six-piece solid-gold table service, and various jewels, using envelopes stamped 'Official' through diplomatic facilities to relations across the Atlantic. They returned in person to the United States the following month.

Only when the Landgravine and Sophie met the commanding officer who had succeeded Captain Nash at Friedrichshof did they learn to their horror that the jewellery was now missing. Given that what had been seized belonged to the family in a private capacity, and as such did not constitute Nazi assets, the Landgravine was aware that it could not be legally confiscated. She contacted the provost marshal in Frankfurt, filed a claim for the return of the missing items, and the Army's Criminal Investigation Division accordingly launched an investigation at once. It became obvious that Captain Nash, Major Watson, and Colonel Durant were responsible.

Within a few weeks, the Criminal Investigation Division agents had caught up with the three suspects. Watson was apprehended in Germany, while Durant and Nash, who had been married on 28 May, were arrested at the La Salle Hotel in Chicago five days later, and charged with being absent without leave, larceny, fraud against the government, conduct unbecoming an officer and a gentleman, and bringing discredit on the military service. Their wedding had been carefully timed, as they knew that a husband and wife could refuse to testify against each other in court-martial proceedings. Nash also hoped to be given judicial immunity on account of her expected honourable discharge from the army. Unbeknown to her, the army had cancelled her separation orders in light of the investigation, so that she remained on active duty, and thus subject to court-martial jurisdiction. A few days later, nearly a million dollars' worth in recovered Hesse family treasure, which the army tried to insist was a trifling amount when compared to the total value of the missing property, was displayed at the Pentagon. Soon afterwards, the Durants were extradited to Germany and flown to Frankfurt to face trial by court-martial. The American authorities were anxious to maintain effective relations and cooperation with their German counterparts, and as such to demonstrate their enforcement of legal accountability among their own servicemen.

Proceedings opened at Frankfurt in June with a tribunal consisting of ten colonels. The recovered jewels were displayed on a long table covered with red velvet. As owner of some of the missing items, Prince August Wilhelm joined the Landgravine, his aunt, to submit detailed evidence about the property. They were both required to identify each of the missing pieces, and testify under oath as to who was the rightful owner. The defence tried to discredit August Wilhelm and his statements on the grounds that he, like his aunt, had been a member of the Nazi party, but the court ruled that political party membership did not disprove witness credibility. The Landgravine, who was very well-informed about jewellery and naturally well acquainted with the history and provenance of the family possessions, impressed the court with her testimony and knowledge of the individual pieces. From his cell at Darmstadt, where he had been interned pending his trial for alleged war crimes, Philipp was also brought before the court to confirm that the pieces were owned by the Hesse-Cassel family (as opposed to the Darmstadt branch of the family).[24] The question of legal ownership was complicated by whether the stolen articles were *Kronjuwelen* (crown jewels), and therefore state assets, or *Familienschmuck* (family jewels), and thus private family property.

In their defence, Watson and the Durants claimed that the items had been owned by people who were dead, SS members or 'ardent' Nazi party members, and therefore there was no prospect of the property ever being returned to them. Although leading party figures had had their property seized, this was not in accordance to American policy. The accused also declared that they were aware that other thefts had taken place at Kronberg, and that collecting souvenirs was so commonplace among GIs that they themselves had done nothing unusual. Nevertheless, the court maintained that there was a difference between souvenirs and highly valuable jewellery of considerable historical interest. The defendants admitted to having removed diamonds and other gems from their settings, and thus considerably reduced their value, especially in the case of items from the eighteenth century.

Captain Nash Durant's defence counsel claimed that the court had no authority over her because the army had rescinded her separation orders for the sole purpose of maintaining jurisdiction over her. He also argued that, even if this was not the case, his client was not guilty of any offences involving the Hesse crown jewels on the grounds that the family had abandoned the treasures and the jewels were legitimate spoils of war. To this the trial counsel answered that they were obliged to ensure that any private property in occupied enemy territory was respected, and that any interference with private property for personal gain would be justly punished. Watson maintained that looting was common in Germany and that, as the treasure belonged either to dead Nazi party or SS members, the property could not be returned to them. In his summary to the panel, the trial counsel reminded the court that there were people who took advantage of abnormal conditions in occupied Germany, but that millions of soldiers went through the war without yielding to similar temptation.

The trial lasted for about a year and was concluded in July 1947. The court found Nash Durant guilty, and sentenced her to five years in jail and dismissal. The court found Watson not guilty of larceny, but convicted him of the remaining offences, including receiving stolen property. He was sentenced to three years in jail and dismissal. In a court martial convened in Frankfurt but concluded in Washington DC, Colonel Durant was found guilty of all charges, and sentenced to fifteen years in prison and dismissal. They served their sentences at the Disciplinary Barracks, Fort Leavenworth, Kansas. Watson was paroled later that year and died in 1984, while the other two were released in 1952. Nash Durant died in 1983, and Durant a year later, both from alcohol-related illnesses.

The end of the trial did not conclude the Hesse-Cassel family's troubles. They were initially denied custody of the recovered jewels, which were sent to Washington DC as evidence in an additional civil trial. Some observers reckoned that they might simply be absorbed by the American administration and their value counted against war reparations. Major Robinson, one of the American attorneys at the Frankfurt trial, offered to represent the Landgravine and her family for a fee of 25 per cent of the jewels' value, which after some deliberation she and the family agreed to accept.

Early in 1951, the American government decided to restore the jewels to the family. This was made conditional on the prior settlement of Major Robinson's fee, and as there were two very different appraisals of the jewels' estimated value, there were long-drawn-out negotiations. The higher figure was eventually settled on and Robinson chose the most valuable objects to take them back to the United States as part of his fee. The rest of the valuables were flown by special aircraft to Frankfurt on 1 August. Involved in the turnover were twenty-two army safes, each measuring a cubic foot, containing over 270 articles. Among the articles were a platinum bracelet encrusted with 405 diamonds, a platinum watch and bracelet with 606 diamonds, a sapphire weighing 116 carats, a group of diamonds weighing 283 carats, and a gold bracelet with 27 diamonds, 54 rubies and 67 emeralds.

The European Army Command announced the return of the Hesse jewels to their owners in an official press release on the day of their transferal, commending the cooperation of the Department of the Army and the Department of the Treasury for this result. According to Wolfgang, they recovered only about a tenth of what had been stolen, though this has been disputed by other sources. Various pieces emerged on the market over the next few decades, many of them 'souvenirs' which had found their way to America. Some were returned to the family by descendants of those who had removed or acquired them, but to this day many still remain unaccounted for. More than half the Hesse crown jewels, and most of the gold and silver that had been hidden in the wine cellar, were never recovered.

The Hesse-Cassels were distressed by the long affair, but this did not stop them from befriending some of the Americans with whom it brought them into contact. Many of the United States officers and soldiers based in Germany had the utmost respect for 'Tante Mossy', the woman whom they soon came to regard as 'a welcome guest, oftentimes a candid and friendly adviser, and a source of unique recollections and historical reminiscences'.[25] Some of them assisted in the reburial of the remains of King Friedrich Wilhelm I and Friedrich II ('the Great') of Prussia; when a GI asked her whether the reburials had been carried out in a 'dignified and appropriate' fashion, she is recorded to have replied that not even her own people could have done better.[26]

Philipp was moved from captivity in Dachau by the Americans, but as a former Nazi official, he was re-arrested and sentenced to another three years in internment camps before being released in 1948. For the rest of his life, he devoted himself to preserving the property and artistic heritage of the family. He had the chapel at Friedrichshof—destroyed in an air-raid—rebuilt to accommodate his brothers' and their father's remains once more. In 1953, Friedrichshof was returned to the family, although his mother remained in the rooms which the American army had allowed her after they had taken over.

In the post-war world, the younger members of the family recognised that it was not practicable to maintain the house as a family home any more than it had been in the harsh economic climate of the 1920s. A decision was made to turn it into a luxury hotel, while retaining and disturbing as little as possible the Empress Frederick's rooms and collections. Many of the smaller items had been pilfered, but some larger artefacts, paintings and pieces of furniture too large to steal had not been moved.

In October 1951, the Landgravine wrote to Queen Mary and King George VI to ask whether he might authorise the return of Queen Victoria's letters; the Viennese biographer Conte Egon Caesar Corti had expressed a wish to study and make use of them for a prospective biography of Kaiser Friedrich and Empress Frederick. They were duly sent back two months later in a specially made crate. Corti began his work the following year, but his health was failing and he died in September 1953, leaving the project unfinished. The Landgravine undertook to revise his draft, but after approving his first two chapters, she became ill herself and did not live long enough to complete the task. Still residing in the estate manager's house, she died on 22 January 1954, the fifty-third anniversary of her grandmother Queen Victoria's death, who also died aged eighty-one. Margaret's body lay in state in the entrance hall at Friedrichshof, and after the funeral, she was laid to rest in the chapel alongside her husband and her sons.

Corti's biography, entitled *Wenn* (*If*), was completed by others. It was published in Germany in 1955, and an English translation, *The English Empress*, followed two years later. Ownership of the correspondence at Kronberg passed from the Landgravine to her son Philipp. After devoting the final years of his life to artistic and cultural pursuits, he died in 1980. He had lived to see four volumes of his grandmother and great-grandmother's exchanges edited by the British author and historian Roger Fulford, and the first volume, *Dearest Child*, published in 1964. Fulford, who was awarded a knighthood towards the end of his life, died in 1982, shortly after publishing the fifth volume of letters, *Beloved Mama*. The series was concluded in 1990 with the appearance of *Beloved and darling child*, edited by Agatha Ramm.

Though only six years had separated the three in age, the Landgravine had survived her two closest sisters by almost quarter of a century. One of them became a Queen Consort and died in exile, while another might have become a Princess Consort and followed the same trajectory. Margaret herself might have married a son of King Edward VII and given England a king, or married a tsarevich and given the Russian Empire healthy male heirs, or she could have become the first Queen of Finland. All three sisters had known great sadness in their adult lives. One had made a second marriage that wavered between farce and tragedy, and culminated in her humiliation and poverty; one had seen her husband forced to relinquish his throne twice and lost a son in pitiful circumstances; and one, who had seen her country defeated in not one, but two world wars, had lived long enough to witness the occupation of her home, and the wanton removal and illegal dispersal of many treasured family heirlooms. Despite the tragedy and misfortune that marked their lives, the three sisters had strived to serve their country and their family.

Notes

Abbreviations:

EF—Crown Princess of Prussia, later Empress Victoria, then Empress Frederick
HC—Hilda Chichester, later Lady Corkran
PMLH—Princess Margaret of Prussia, later Landgravine of Hesse
PLB—Princess Louis of Battenberg, formerly Princess Victoria of Hesse
PVP—Princess Victoria of Prussia
QV—Queen Victoria

Chapter 1

1. Victoria of Prussia, *My memoirs*, p. 2.
2. *Letters of the Empress Frederick*, p. 59, EF to QV, 19.5.1866.
3. Victoria, Queen, *Your Dear Letter*, p. 77, EF to QV, 19.6.1866.
4. *Ibid.*, pp. 80-1, EF to QV, 16.7.1866.
5. *Ibid.*, p. 136, EF to QV, 13.5.1867.
6. *Ibid.*, p. 137, QV to EF, 18.5.1867.
7. *Ibid.*, p. 195, EF to QV, 10.6.1868.
8. Victoria, Queen, *Your Dear Letter*, p. 196; EF to QV, 10.6.1868.
9. *Ibid.*, p. 276, EF to QV, 29.4.1870.
10. *Letters of the Empress Frederick*, p. 80, EF to QV, 25.7.1870.
11. Pakula, p. 297, EF to QV, 8.3.1872.
12. Victoria, Queen, *Darling Child*, p. 37; Pakula, p. 297, QV to EF, 10.3.1872.
13. *Ibid.*, p. 39, EF to QV, 3.5.1872.
14. Victoria, Queen, *Darling Child*, p. 39, EF to QV, 3.5.1872.

15. Victoria, Queen, *Beloved Mama*, p. 88, EF to QV, 22.4.1873.
16. *Ibid.*, pp. 74-5, EF to QV, 22.4.1880.
17. Victoria of Prussia, *My Memoirs*, p. 3.
18. *Ibid.*, p. 5.
19. Victoria, Queen, *Beloved Mama*, p. 106, EF to QV, 25.8.1881.
20. Victoria of Prussia, *My memoirs*, pp. 6-7.
21. *Ibid.*, p. 8.
22. *Ibid.*, pp. 16-7.
23. Victoria, Queen, *Darling Child*, p. 284, EF to QV, 1.1.1878.
24. Victoria of Prussia, *My memoirs*, p. 9.
25. *Ibid.*, pp. 21-2.
26. Victoria, Queen, *Beloved Mama*, p. 86, EF to QV, 7.8.180, 10.8.80.
27. Victoria of Prussia, *My memoirs*, p. 22.

Chapter 2

1. *Corti, Downfall of three dynasties*, pp. 270-1.
2. Epton, p. 166.
3. Corti, *Alexander von Battenberg*, p. 74.
4. Corti, *Downfall of three dynasties*, p. 289.
5. Corti, *Alexander von Battenberg*, pp. 88-9.
6. Clark, p. 15.
7. William II, p. 263.
8. Corti, *Alexander von Battenberg*, p. 96.
9. *Ibid.*, p. 107.
10. Corti, *Downfall of three dynasties*, p. 303.
11. Victoria, Queen, *Beloved Mama*, p. 88, PVP to QV, 24.12.1884.
12. Corti, *Alexander von Battenberg*, p. 148.
13. *Ibid., p.* 149.
14. *Corti, English Empress*, p. 226, QV to EF, 10.1.1885.
15. *McClintock, p. 237.*
16. Ibid., p. 237.
17. *Corti, Downfall of three dynasties*, p. 305, Prince of Bulgaria to Prince Alexander of Hesse, 22.2.1885.
18. Corti, *Alexander von Battenberg*, p. 239.
19. *Ibid.*, p. 241.
20. Corti, *Downfall of three dynasties*, p. 323.
21. Corti, *Alexander von Battenberg*, pp. 253-4.
22. Corti, *Downfall of three dynasties*, p. 343.
23. Victoria of Prussia, *My memoirs*, p. 74.
24. Corti, *Downfall of three dynasties*, p. 333.

25. *Ibid.*, p. 334.
26. Steinberg, pp. 35-6.
27. Longford, p. 506.
28. PVP to Mrs Talbot, 5.4.1888, Private collection.
29. *Letters of the Empress Frederick*, p. 316, EF to QV, 15.6.1888.
30. Hough, p. 144, QV to PLB, 4.7.1888.
31. Corti, *Alexander von Battenberg*, p. 298.
32. *Ibid.*, pp. 298-9.
33. Victoria, Queen, *Beloved and darling child*, p. 74, QV to EF, 17.7.1888.
34. Corti, *English Empress*, p. 313.
35. Victoria, Queen, *Beloved and darling child*, p. 77, QV to EF, 4.9.1888.
36. *Letters of the Empress Frederick*, p. 319, EF to QV, 18.6.1888.
37. Victoria, Queen, *Letters 1886-1901*, Vol 1, p. 443, QV to Lord Salisbury, 24.10.1888.
38. Röhl, *Wilhelm II, personal monarchy*, p. 66, EF to Emperor William II, 7 11 1888.
39. Alice, p. 70.
40. Victoria, Queen, *Advice to a grand-daughter*, p. 100, QV to PLB, 31.3.1889.
41. Victoria, Queen, *Beloved and darling child*, 88-9, EF to QV, 30.5.1889; *Queen Victoria at Windsor and Balmoral*, p. 26.
42. Victoria, Queen, *Beloved and darling child*, pp. 88-9, EF to QV, 30.5.1889.
43. *Queen Victoria at Windsor and Balmoral*, p. 29, PVP to EF, 1.6.1889.
44. Mager, p. 114.
45. Pakula, p. 537, QV to EF, 18.6.1889.
46. *Ibid.*, p. 537, PVP to EF, 19.6.1889.
47. *Ibid., p. 538, EF to QV, 21.6.1889.*

Chapter 3

1. *Letters of the Empress Frederick*, p. 393, EF to QV, 27.10.1889.
2. Nicholas of Greece, *Fifty years*, p. 96.
3. *Letters of the Empress Frederick*, p. 393, EF to QV, 27.10.1889.
4. *Empress Frederick writes to Sophie*, p. 52.
5. *The Times*, 1.4.1890.
6. *Empress Frederick writes to Sophie*, p. 66.
7. Victoria of Prussia, *My memoirs*, p. 112.
8. Victoria, Queen, *Beloved and darling child*, p. 111, EF to QV, 12.6.1890.

9. *Empress Frederick writes to Sophie,* p. 67.
10. Victoria, Queen, *Beloved and darling child,* p. 112, QV to EF, 14.6.1890.
11. Röhl, *Wilhelm II, personal monarchy,* pp. 641-2, Empress Augusta Victoria to Emperor William II, 21.7.1890.
12. Victoria, Queen, *Advice to a grand-daughter,* p. 107, QV to PLB, 15.7.1890.
13. *Empress Frederick writes to Sophie,* p. 59.
14. Victoria, Queen, *Beloved and darling child,* p. 113, QV to EF, 20.7.1890.
15. Röhl, *Wilhelm II, personal monarchy,* p. 642, 10.9.1890.
16. *Ibid.,* p. 115, EF to QV, 31.10.1890.
17. Marie Louise, p. 67 (Princess Marie Louise stated in her account that the wedding feast and torchlight procession did take place, so she may have been confusing this ceremony with another wedding at Berlin at around the same time).
18. Poore, pp. 115-6.
19. Röhl, *Wilhelm II, Personal monarchy,* p. 643.
20. Victoria of Prussia, *My memoirs,* p. 116.
21. Corti, *English Empress,* pp. 337-8.
22. *Empress Frederick writes to Sophie,* p. 76.
23. *Ibid.,* p. 86.
24. Corti, *English Empress,* p. 338, QV to Queen Olga, 13.4.1891.
25. *Ibid.,* p. 339, Emperor William II to QV, 13.5.1891.
26. Röhl, *Wilhelm II, Personal monarchy,* p. 512.
27. *Ibid.,* p. 165, PVP to EF, 9.5.1891.
28. *Ibid.,* pp. 646-8.
29. *Ibid.,* p. 648.
30. *Ibid.,* p. 636.
31. *Ibid.,* p. 648.
32. Victoria of Prussia, *My memoirs,* pp. 52-3.
33. *Royalty Digest,* Vol 11, September 2001, p. 86.
34. *Empress Frederick writes to Sophie,* p. 85.
35. *Ibid.,* p. 93.
36. Victoria of Prussia, *My memoirs,* p. 125.
37. *Empress Frederick writes to Sophie,* p. 112.
38. Victoria of Prussia, *My memoirs,* p. 130.
39. Röhl, *Wilhelm II, Personal monarchy,* p. 122.
40. *Ibid.,* p. 650.
41. St Aubyn, p. 106.
42. *Illustrated London News,* 28.1.1893.
43. Corti, *English Empress,* p. 344, EF to PMLH, 17.5.1892.

44. Victoria, Queen, *Beloved and darling child,* p. 143, EF to QV, 20.6.1892.
45. *Ibid.,* p. 114, QV to EF, 22.6.1890.
46. Röhl, *Wilhelm II, Personal monarchy,* p. 652, p. 654.
47. *Ibid.,* p. 651.
48. Bennett, p. 306.
49. Petropoulos, p. 34.
50. *The Graphic,* 7.1.1893.
51. *Empress Frederick writes to Sophie,* p. 137.
52. *Freeman's Journal & Daily Commercial Advertiser,* 26.1.1893.
53. *Empress Frederick writes to Sophie,* p. 138.
54. Poore, p. 149.
55. *Ibid.,* p. 149.
56. *Fischer,* p. 289.

Chapter 4

1. *Röhl, Wilhelm II, Personal monarchy,* p. 639, EF to PVP, 19.10.1893.
2. *Empress Frederick writes to Sophie,* p. 157.
3. Fontenoy.
4. Victoria, Queen, *Beloved and darling child,* p. 93, QV to EF, 21.4.1893.
5. *Empress Frederick writes to Sophie,* p. 157.
6. *Ibid.,* p. 178.
7. *Ibid.,* p. 195.
8. Röhl, *Wilhelm II, Personal monarchy,* p. 802.
9. Victoria, Queen, *Beloved and darling child,* p. 181, QV to EF, 6.10.1895.
10. Gelardi, pp. 75-6.
11. Victoria, Queen, *Letters 1886-1901,* Vol 3, p. 121, EF to QV, 16.1.1897.
12. *Ibid.,* p. 131, Lord Salisbury to QV, 12.2.1897.
13. *Ibid.,* p. 136, EF to QV, 19.2.1897.
14. Röhl, *Wilhelm II, Personal monarchy,* p. 124.
15. Victoria, Queen, *Letters 1886-1901,* Vol 3, p. 138, QV to Lord Salisbury, 21.2.1897.
16. *Empress Frederick writes to Sophie,* p. 245.
17. *Ibid.,* p. 250.
18. Bülow, *Memoirs 1897-1903,* p. 217.
19. *Empress Frederick writes to Sophie,* p. 295.
20. Mallet, p. 139, 14.10.1898.
21. Victoria, Queen, *Beloved and darling child,* p. 206, QV to EF,

5.8.1897.

22. Gelardi, p. 88.
23. Dugdale, p. 164.
24. Bennett, p. 331.
25. Ponsonby, p. 109.
26. Bennett, p. 331.
27. Epton, p. 225.
28. Victoria of Prussia, *My memoirs,* p. 156.
29. *Empress Frederick writes to Sophie,* pp. 309-10.

Chapter 5

1. *Victoria of Prussia, My memoirs,* p. 157.
2. Gelardi, p. 102, Crown Princess Sophie to unknown correspondent, 26.8.1901.
3. Marie, *Dearest Missy,* p. 346, Crown Princess Marie to Duchess of Saxe-Coburg, 8.8.1898.
4. Bülow, *Memoirs 1903-1909,* pp. 121-2.
5. *The Times,* 18.8.1906.
6. James, p. 111, 15.8.1936.
7. Topham, p. 156.
8. PMLH to HC, 27.9.1910, Bodleian Library, University of Oxford MSS 364/35.
9. Petropoulos, p. 37.
10. Anon, *Recollections,* p. 180.
11. Vickers, p. 107, Nona Kerr to PLB, 10.1.1913.
12. Papacosma, p. 172.
13. PMLH to HC, 19.8.1910, Bodleian Library, University of Oxford MSS 364/37.
14. Gelardi, p. 167, Sir Francis Elliot to Sir Edward Grey, 8.2.1911.
15. *Ibid.,* p. 167, Sir Francis Elliot to Sir Edward Grey, 12.2.1912.
16. *Ibid.,* p. 168.
17. Vickers, p. 103, Nona Kerr to PLB, 25.1.1913.
18. *Ibid.,* p. 108, Nona Kerr to PLB, 25.1.1913.
19. *Ibid.,* p. 108, Nona Kerr to PLB, 27.12.1912.
20. Victoria of Prussia, *My memoirs,* p. 172.
21. PMLH to HC, 4.6.1910, Bodleian Library, University of Oxford MSS 364/27.
22. PMLH to HC, 2.11.1911, Bodleian Library, University of Oxford MSS 364/65.
23. *The Times,* 14.8, 16.8, 21.8, 28.8.1912.

24. Gelardi, p. 192, PMLH to HC, 3.4.1913.
25. PMLH to HC, 31.3.1913, Bodleian Library, University of Oxford MSS 364/91.
26. PMLH to HC, 20.5.1913, Bodleian Library, University of Oxford MSS 364/101.
27. PMLH to HC, 10.6.1913, Bodleian Library, University of Oxford MSS 364/103.
28. Petropoulos, p. 39.

Chapter 6

1. PMLH to HC, 26.1.1915, Bodleian Library, University of Oxford MSS 364/145.
2. PMLH to HC, 30.12.1915, Bodleian Library, University of Oxford MSS 364/148.
3. Petropoulos, p. 44.
4. PMLH to HC, 2.12.1916, Bodleian Library, University of Oxford MSS 364/151.
5. Victoria of Prussia, *My memoirs*, p. 184.
6. *Ibid.*, p. 186.
7. *Ibid.*, p. 192.
8. Nicolson, p. 282, King George V to Sir Edward Grey, 4.9.1916.
9. Gelardi, p. 249, PMLH to HC, 3.12.1915.
10. *Ibid.*, p. 250.
11. Nicholas of Greece, *Political memoirs*, p. 263-4.
12. Gelardi, PMLH to HC, p. 276.
13. Petropoulos, pp. 54-5.
14. Röhl, *Wilhelm II, Into the abyss*, p. 1195.

Chapter 7

1. Petropoulos, p. 83.
2. Nicholas, p. 152.
3. Victoria of Prussia, *My memoirs*, p. 194.
4. Wheeler-Bennett, p. 121.
5. Ziegler, p. 85, Prince of Wales to Queen Mary, 8.1.1919.
6. Victoria of Prussia, *My memoirs*, p. 198.
7. ibid, p. 208.
8. Röhl, *Wilhelm II, Into the abyss*, p. 1201.
9. PMLH to HC, 17.11.1919, Bodleian Library, University of Oxford

MSS 364/157.

10. Christopher, p. 153.
11. Gelardi, p. 308, PMLH to HC, 6.12.1920.
12. Prince George of Greece to Grand Duchess Xenia of Russia, 2.11.1920, Private collection.
13. Christopher, p. 172.
14. Gelardi, p. 312, PMLH to HC, 3.3.1921.
15. *Ibid.*, p. 315, PMLH to HC, 28.5.1922.
16. Eulalia, p. 56.
17. *Royalty Digest*, Vol 14, Oct 2004, pp. 112-3, Mrs Whitaker, 29.12.1922.
18. Victoria of Prussia, *My memoirs*, p. 210.
19. *Ibid.*, p. 16, p. 212.
20. *Ibid.*, p. 214.
21. Wheeler-Bennett, p. 194.
22. Elsberry, p. 174.
23. Minet, *Even more reading....*
24. Nicholas, pp. 114-5.
25. Christopher, p. 260 (Prince Christopher stated that this conversation took place at a wedding in October 1932, but Queen Sophie had died earlier that year, and it was more probably that of Princess Olga of Greece to Prince Paul of Yugoslavia in October 1923).
26. Alexandra, *For a King's love,* p. 21; Alexandra, *Prince Philip*, p. 39.

Chapter 8

1. Victoria of Prussia, *My memoirs*, p. 242.
2. The *Times,* 11.10.1927.
3. *Ibid.*, 20.11.1927.
4. Victoria of Prussia, *My memoirs*, p. 243.
5. The *Times,* 25.2.1928.
6. Rosvall, *Sasja.*
7. *Baltimore Sun*, February 1928.
8. Van der Kiste, *Crowns in a changing world*, p. 173, Queen Sophie to King George V, 15.3.1928.
9. Cecil, Vol 2, p. 10.
10. *The Times*, 28.11.1928.
11. *Ibid.*, 7.6.1929.
12. Victoria of Prussia, *My memoirs*, p. 74.
13. *Ibid.*, p. 182.
14. *Ibid.*, p. 172.

15. *Ibid.*, p. 199.
16. Ponsonby, p. 112.
17. PMLH to HC, 1.11.1928, Bodleian Library, University of Oxford MSS 365/38.
18. Ponsonby, pp. 114-5.
19. Victoria Louise, p. 27.
20. *The Times*, 26.9.1929, 4.10.1929.
21. Rosvall, *Sasja*.
22. *The Times*, 29.1.1936.
23. PMLH to HC, 10.5.1931, Bodleian Library, University of Oxford MSS 365/76.
24. Alexandra, *For a King's love*, p. 25.
25. Gelardi, p. 373, PMLH to HC, 17.12.31.
26. MLH to HC, 6.1.1932, Bodleian Library, University of Oxford MSS 365/86.
27. *Ibid.*, p. 374, PMLH to HC, 23.2.1932.
28. Gelardi, p. 374, Princess Irene of Greece to Irina Procopiou, 21.3.1932.
29. Victoria Louise, p. 189.
30. *The Times,* 18.1.1932.
31. Gelardi, p. 374, PMLH to HC, 17.12.1935.

Chapter 9

1. Hart-Davis, pp. 278-9, 27.10.1922.
2. MLH to HC, 17.5.1932, Bodleian Library, University of Oxford MSS 364/91.
3. MLH to HC, 25.4.1933, Bodleian Library, University of Oxford MSS 364/101.
4. Petropoulos, pp. 104-5.
5. Röhl, *Kaiser and his Court*, p. 15.
6. Balfour, p. 419.
7. Röhl, *Wilhelm II, Into the abyss*, p. 1263.
8. Petropoulos, p. 108.
9. Rose, p. 229, King George V to Ernst, Duke of Hesse, 16.5.1935.
10. MLH to HC, 19.12.1936, Bodleian Library, University of Oxford MSS 364/153.

11. MLH to HC, 2.6.1937, Bodleian Library, University of Oxford MSS 364/158.
12. MLH to HC, 2.5.1937, Bodleian Library, University of Oxford MSS

364/155.

13. MLH to HC, 30.9.1938, Bodleian Library, University of Oxford MSS 364/189.

14. MLH to HC, 29.4.1939, Bodleian Library, University of Oxford MSS 364/205.

15. Victoria Louise, pp. 200-1.

16. Petropoulos, p. 103, PMLH to Adolf Hitler, 3.6.1940.

17. Bradford, p. 425.

18. Petropoulos, p. 226.

19. Röhl, *Kaiser and his Court*, p. 211, ex-Emperor William II to PMLH, 3.11.1940.

20. Vickers, p. 301, PLB to Nona Kerr, 16.10.1943 .

21. Petropoulos, pp. 316-7.

22. Pakula, p. 599.

23. Lesley, *'Tante Mossy'*.

24. Petropoulos, p. 351.

Bibliography

Books

The place of publication is London unless otherwise stated

Alexandra, Queen, *For a King's love: The intimate recollections of Queen Alexandra of Yugoslavia* (Odhams, 1956)

—*Prince Philip: A family portrait* (Hodder & Stoughton, 1960)

Alice, Princess, *For my grandchildren: Some reminiscences of H.R.H. Princess Alice, Countess of Athlone* (Evans Bros, 1966)

Anon., *Recollections of three Kaisers* (Herbert Jenkins, 1929)

Balfour, Michael, *The Kaiser and his times* (Cresset, 1964)

Bennett, Daphne, *Vicky, Princess Royal of England and German Empress* (Collins Harvill, 1971)

Bradford, Sarah, *George VI* (Weidenfeld & Nicolson, 1989)

Bülow, Prince von, *Memoirs 1897-1903* (Putnam, 1931)

  Memoirs 1903-1909 (Putnam, 1931)

Bunsen, Marie von, *The world I used to know* (Thornton Butterworth, 1930)

Carter, Miranda, *Anthony Blunt: His lives* (Macmillan, 2001)

Cecil, Lamar, *Wilhelm II, Vol. 1: Prince and Emperor, 1859-1900* (Chapel Hill: University of North Carolina, 1989)

—*Wilhelm II, Vol. 2: Emperor and Exile, 1900-1941* (Chapel Hill: University of North Carolina, 1996)

Clark, Christopher, *Kaiser Wilhelm II: A life in power* (Penguin, 2009)

Corti, Egon Caesar Conte, *Alexander von Battenberg* (Cassell, 1954)

—*The downfall of three dynasties* (Cassell, 1934)

—*The English Empress: A study in the relations between Queen Victoria and her eldest Daughter, Empress Frederick of Germany* (Cassell, 1957)

Dugdale, Edgar T. S., *Maurice de Bunsen: Diplomat and friend* (John

Murray, 1934)

Elsberry, Terence, *Marie of Romania: The intimate life of a twentieth-century Queen* (Cassell, 1973)

Epton, Nina, *Victoria and her daughters* (Weidenfeld & Nicolson, 1971)

Eulalia, Infanta, *Courts and countries after the war* (New York: Dodd, Mead, 1925)

Fischer, Henry W., *The private lives of William II & his Consort: A secret history of the court of Berlin* (Heinemann, 1904)

Fontenoy, Mme La Marquise de (Marguerite Cunliffe-Owen), *The Secret Memoirs of the Courts of Europe: William II, Germany; Francis Joseph, Austria-Hungary* (Philadelphia, Barrie, 1900) http://www.fullbooks.com/The-Secret-Memoirs-of-the-Courts-of-Europe1.html (accessed January 2014)

Gelardi, Julia P., *Born to rule: Granddaughters of Victoria, Queens of Europe* (Headline, 2004)

Gould Lee, Arthur S., *The royal house of Greece* (Ward Lock, 1948)

Hart-Davis, Rupert, ed., *Siegfried Sassoon diaries, 1920-1922* (Faber, 1981)

Hough, Richard, *Louis and Victoria: The first Mountbattens* (Hutchinson, 1974)

Hourmouzios, Stelio, *No ordinary crown: A biography of King Paul of the Hellenes* (Weidenfeld & Nicolson, 1972)

James, Robert Rhodes, ed., *'Chips': The diaries of Sir Henry Channon* (Phoenix, 1996)

Longford, Elizabeth, *Victoria R.I.* (Weidenfeld & Nicolson, 1964)

Lynx, J. J., *The great Hohenzollern scandal* (Oldbourne, 1965)

Lytton, Lady, *Lady Lytton's Court Diary 1895-1899* (Rupert Hart-Davis, 1961)

Mager, Hugo, *Elizabeth, Grand Duchess of Russia* (New York: Carroll & Graf, 1998)

Mallet, Victor, ed., *Life with Queen Victoria: Marie Mallet's letters from court, 1887-1901* (John Murray, 1968)

Marie, Duchess of Edinburgh, *Dearest Missy: The correspondence between Marie, Grand Duchess of Russia, Duchess of Edinburgh and of Saxe-Coburg and Gotha and her daughter Marie, Crown Princess of Roumania, 1879-1900*, ed. Diana Mandache (Falkoping: Rosvall Royal Books, 2011)

Marie Louise, Princess, *My memories of six reigns* (Evans Bros, 1956)

Nicholas of Greece, Prince, *My fifty years* (Hutchinson, 1926)

  Political memoirs: Pages from my diary (Hutchinson, 1928)

Nichols, Beverley, *25: Being a young man's candid recollection of his elders and betters* (Jonathan Cape, 1926)

Pakula, Hannah, *An uncommon woman: The Empress Frederick*

(Weidenfeld & Nicolson, 1996)

Papacosma, S. Victor, *The military in Greek politics: The 1909 coup d'état* (Kent, OH: Kent State University Press, 1977)

Petropoulos, Jonathan, *Royals and the Reich: The Princes von Hessen in Nazi Germany* (New York: Oxford University Press, 2006)

Ponsonby, Sir Frederick, *Recollections of three reigns* (Eyre & Spottiswoode, 1951)

Poore, Judith U., *The memoirs of Emily Loch, Discretion in waiting: Tsarina Alexandra and the Christian family* (Kinloss: Librario, 2007)

Pope-Hennessy, James, ed., *Queen Victoria at Windsor and Balmoral: Letters from her grand-daughter Princess Victoria of Prussia, June 1889* (Allen & Unwin, 1959)

Reid, Michaela, *Ask Sir James: Sir James Reid, Personal Physician to Queen Victoria and physician-in-ordinary to three monarchs* (Hodder & Stoughton, 1987)

Ridley, Jane, *Bertie: A life of Edward VII* (Chatto & Windus, 2012)

Röhl, John, *The Kaiser and his Court: Wilhelm II and the Government of Germany* (Cambridge University Press, 1996)

—*Wilhelm II: The Kaiser's personal monarchy, 1888-1900* (Cambridge University Press, 2004)

—*Wilhelm II: Into the abyss of war and exile, 1900-1941* (Cambridge University Press, 2014)

—*Young Wilhelm: The Kaiser's early life, 1859-1888* (Cambridge University Press, 1998)

Rose, Kenneth, *King George V* (Weidenfeld & Nicolson, 1983)

St Aubyn, Giles, *Edward VII, Prince and King* (Collins, 1979)

Steinberg, Jonathan, *Bismarck: A life* (Oxford University Press, 2011)

Topham, Anne, *A distant thunder* (New York: New Chapter Press, 1992)

Van der Kiste, John, *Crowns in a changing world: The British and European monarchies 1901-36* (Stroud: Sutton, 1993)

—*Dearest Vicky, Darling Fritz: Queen Victoria's eldest daughter and the German Emperor* (Stroud: Sutton, 2001)

—*Kaiser Wilhelm II: Germany's last Emperor* (Stroud: Sutton, 1999)

—*Kings of the Hellenes: The Greek Kings 1863-1974* (Stroud: Sutton, 1994)

Vickers, Hugo, *Alice, Princess Andrew of Greece* (Viking, 2000)

Victoria, Consort of Frederick III, German Emperor, *The Empress Frederick writes to Sophie*, ed. Arthur Gould Lee (Faber, 1955)

—*Letters of the Empress Frederick,* ed. Sir Frederick Ponsonby (Macmillan, 1928)

Victoria, Queen, *The Letters of Queen Victoria, 2nd Series: a Selection from Her Majesty's Correspondence and Journal between the years 1862 and 1885*, ed. G. E. Buckle, 3 vols (John Murray, 1926-8)

—*The Letters of Queen Victoria, 3rd Series: a Selection from Her Majesty's*

Correspondence and Journal between the years 1886 and 1901, ed. G. E. Buckle, 3 vols (John Murray, 1930-2)

—*Dearest Mama: Private Correspondence of Queen Victoria and the Crown Princess of Prussia, 1861-1864;* ed. Roger Fulford (Evans Bros, 1968)

—*Your Dear Letter: Private Correspondence of Queen Victoria and the Crown Princess of Prussia, 1865-1871,* ed. Roger Fulford (Evans Bros, 1971)

—*Darling Child: Private Correspondence of Queen Victoria and the Crown Princess of Prussia, 1871-1878;* ed. Roger Fulford (Evans Bros, 1976)

—*Beloved Mama: Private Correspondence of Queen Victoria and the German Crown Princess of Prussia, 1878-1885;* ed. Roger Fulford (Evans Bros, 1981)

—*Beloved and Darling Child: Last letters Queen Victoria and her eldest daughter, 1886-1901;* ed. Agatha Ramm (Stroud: Sutton, 1990)

—*Advice to a grand-daughter: Letters from Queen Victoria to Princess Victoria of Hesse,* ed. Richard Hough (Heinemann, 1975)

Victoria of Prussia, Princess, *My memoirs,* (Eveleigh, Nash & Grayson, 1929; *Royalty Digest,* 1995)

Victoria Louise, Princess, *The Kaiser's daughter: Memoirs,* ed. Robert Vacha, (W.H. Allen, 1977)

Vovk, Justin C., *Imperial requiem: Four royal women and the fall of the age of empires* (Bloomington: Universe, 2012)

Wheeler-Bennett, John W., *King George VI, His life and reign* (Macmillan, 1958)

William II, Ex-Emperor, *My early life* (Methuen, 1926)

Ziegler, Philip, *King Edward VIII: The official biography* (Collins, 1990)

Journals

Baltimore Sun
Freeman's Journal & Daily Commercial Advertiser
Illustrated London News
New York Times
Royalty Digest
The Graphic
The Standard
The Times

Articles

Eilers, Marlene, 'Landgraf Moritz of Hesse', *European Royal History Journal*, XCIII
'Queen Sophie of Greece, "One of the best of women"', *Royalty Digest*, Vol. II, February 1993

Horbury, David, 'A tragic princess: Princess Victoria of Prussia', *Royalty Digest*, Vol. VI, March, April and May 1997 (three parts)

Lesley, Parker, 'Tante Mossy', *Times Literary Supplement*, 2846, 14 September 1956

Minet, Paul, 'Even more reading between the lines: Some final interpolations by Miss Grizel Gray of Walmer', *Royalty Digest*, Vol. XII, April 2002

Pollock, Kassandra, 'Victoria, Princess of Prussia', *European Royal History Journal*, XXVIII, XXIX (two parts)

Rosvall, Ted, 'Sasja—the charming scoundrel', *Royalty Digest Quarterly* (1/2012)

Van der Kiste, John, 'Princess Margaret of Prussia: The granddaughter who saved Queen Victoria's letters', *Royalty Digest*, Vol. I, June 1992

Zeepvat, Charlotte, 'My darling Friedrichshof', *Royalty Digest*, Vol. XI, August and September 2001 (two parts)
'The Cassel line', *Royalty Digest*, Vol. VI, June 1997

Index